Living in Style

JOCASTA INNES
Living in Style

A COSMOPOLITAN BOOK

IN ASSOCIATION WITH
Ⓘ Dulux

GUILD PUBLISHING
LONDON

Dedicated to my best of all people, Daisy, Jason, Tabitha and Chloe.

Too many to itemise, I would like to thank all those good people who allowed us to move in on them, move the furniture about, make cups of tea and generally disturb domestic peace and order. For kindnesses beyond the call of duty, special citations to Polly Hope, who lent her own photos, Alan Short who drew a plan, Gill Goldsmith who allowed us to rearrange her wonderful house, Delia da Silva ditto, Alison MacDonald who bought armfuls of lilies. On the production front, a big hand for Simon Brown who took most of the pix, Amanda who helped, Anna and David who put it all into shape. Waves of gratitude to Deirdre for being encouraging always, firm when necessary, and to Denny for brilliantly stagemanaging the cover. Pats on the back to Julian, who stencilled, and Fiona Skrine who marbled my fireplace twice over, with saintly patience and great skill. And finally hugs and kisses to my children and to Richard, who put up with me while I was impossible to live with.

Jocasta Innes

This edition published 1984 by
Book Club Associates

By arrangement with Ebury Press
National Magazine House
72 Broadwick Street
London W1V 2BP

Designed by David Fordham

Illustrations by Ivan Ripley

Front cover photographs by Tony Chau

Filmset by Advanced Filmsetters (Glasgow) Ltd.
Printed and bound in Italy by New Interlitho, s.p.a., Milan

INTRODUCTION

Style is such an obligingly stretchy word, meaning all things to all people, that some attempt to define what it means in terms of this book seems necessary. It does not have those exclusive and conformist connotations attached to notions like 'good taste' or 'elegance'. Good taste and elegance can be stylish, but style can ignore these criteria—look at punk fashion. 'It's much better for style to be poor,' insists Stanley Falconer, doyen of decorators. 'Rich people can order taste from a good decorator but that isn't quite the same thing.'

Imaginative problem solving is one feature of style. A couple I know, desperate for storage in their kitchen, happened by a shop selling up and came away with yards of old display cabinets, grubby, panes missing, but solid mahogany. Dennis Severs, the enterprising young American who makes a living showing visitors round his imaginatively restored seventeenth-century house in Spitalfields, needed to smarten up his handsome but battered staircase quickly and hit on the idea of using boot polish, which darkens and burnishes all in one go. It takes more than a few clever ideas to create style, as I shall explain, but the spirit of imaginative common sense which provides such simple, excellent solutions is the spirit which underpins many stylish interiors.

I think we need to distinguish between style and Styles. The latter are transitory looks, often a bit extreme, fun, sparky, stimulating—punk in fashion, high tech or ornamentalist in interiors—but while they are worth trying on, like hats, when one is young and a bit undefined, they have the disadvantage of all exaggerated Styles, they soon date, ossify, whereas you are forever moving on. I think everyone should try freaking out at the stage when black walls and a silver ceiling stuck with luminous stars seems magical. There would be no style, in my sense of the word, if there weren't people cheerfully overturning the aesthetic applecart and taking the risks older, lazier, more sceptical folk tend to shun. For this reason I, and all the designers I admire, treat all these fringe experiments with respect—life is too short to try out all the possible combinations and, approached with an open mind, the dottiest schemes and wildest notions are fascinating and instructive.

Stylish rooms I know tend to be changing a little all the time, a new find taking pride of place, something else banished, pictures getting swapped round, a handy small table finding a home under a window and attracting a chair to it, then books or a workbasket. Then, at longer intervals, the owner suddenly gets a new inspiration, stencils maybe, or a new colour for the walls, or light floating curtains for summer, and everything changes. One quality stylish rooms share—they are never static or sterile or unlived in. Just how hard it is to pin down this lived-in quality everyone who has created room sets for photography well knows. You can take endless trouble to make it look real and convincing, mixing old things among the new, dishevelling flower arrangements and cushions, but a knowing eye can always detect the fraud. A philosopher once defined the soul as the ghost in the machine. In a room set, however inventive or pretty, the machine is just a machine.

Surprisingly perhaps, there seems to be less and less difference between the styles men and women create for themselves. Masculine and feminine styles, in the stereotyped sense, are merging, though men do fight shy of frills, bows and lace and women look a bit lost in the more austerely architectural settings. But many men choose pastel colours for their walls, and many

---

Dennis Severs, presiding with justifiable satisfaction over his achievement, succeeds in mixing real antiques with brilliant stage effects—those 'Grinling Gibbons' type swags are loops of walnuts and dried foliage worked together to help create the atmosphere of an eighteenth century drawing room, while the drifts of lavender and cloves by the skirting boards subtly scent the air.

women opt for cool streamlined modern chic. One distinction that makes more sense to me now is the one between extrovert and introvert styles, what I tend to think of — without value judgment — as warm and cool styles.

Extrovert style is strong on colours, always in the plural, but soft, warm, massed in an impressionist palette. Its outgoing side is underlined by kindly thoughts, like enveloping seats, low lighting, lots of cushions, books, flowers. Extrovert places want to please, charm, rather than surprise or provoke, and their style is personal in a casual, uncontrived way, more an overflowing of interests, than anything thought out. Extroverts collect things, but in a whimsical, impulsive way, not seriously, and their room are like nests feathered with magpie inconsequence, bits and pieces looking a little surprised to find themselves neighbours, but somehow welded together into a place by the owner's powerful presence. Extroverts have no trouble creating atmosphere.

The introverted room is private, a retreat rather than a social stage. What first impresses is space. Introverts have a more selective attitude to things, which they like to be exceptional, rare or in some way significant. Otherwise they should be functional. But either way there will not be many of them. Minimalism appeals here, a chair and lamp being the only indispensable items of furniture in their living space aside from the superb music centre, discs neatly classified, and shelves tightly but neatly packed with mostly paperback books. Bedrooms are basic, possibly a futon on a low platform, kitchens surprisingly well equipped and neat. While these places have an enigmatic, secretive feel to them, 'museums of the soul' to quote Mario Praz, they may incorporate some extraordinary stylistic flourish, often painted so as not to encroach on floor space — a disturbing 'now you see me now you don't' bit of *trompe l'oeil*, a surrealist ceiling, or a random band of stripes which starts at one skirting, arches over the ceiling and down another wall like an angular rainbow. Where extroverts anticipate your comments, rushing to explain, introverts rarely explain anything. One senses, without being told, that the placing of things is ritualized, part of a private iconography. Unaccommodating places these, but often in their cool, freakish way, very stylish.

One of the paradoxes of personal style is that while it changes superficially over the years, recording passing enthusiasms and influences, it usually maintains an inner consistency, the fingerprints of its author coming through everything like the legend on Brighton rock. At least, this is the way once the style itself has clarified, which is usually in a person's early thirties. I have often noticed that in houses which have the assured look of a matured style about them, that you can move things about, from one room or one floor to the next, without them looking out of place. Everything is congruous because it has been chosen by the same selective eye, though for different reasons. In a colourist's house, especially, colours everywhere intermingle like old friends. This continuity of rooms gives a sense of a house as an organism.

THE STYLE

Putting on the Style

Few words are bandied about more freely in this last slice of the twentieth century than style. Style is the special preoccupation of our times. Spotting styles just out of the egg, analysing and classifying them is a media reflex that has become an international parlour game. There are people styles, place styles, nation styles. There is street style, parent to a whole family of much discussed, elaborately differentiated substyles. There is life style, one of those handily stretchy word bags any meaning can be stuffed into, though usually with little stylistic import.

So what are we trying to do when we salt the tail of this protean, elusive quality, immediately recognizable but supposedly indefinable, called style? *The Oxford Dictionary* defines style in terms of form and manner rather than content. Are we then a society obsessed by appearances? Well, yes, to some extent though I think the old French preacher was nearer the mark when he pronounced, '*Le style, c'est l'homme*'—your style is you. The more your style is you the more distinctive it is as a style and implicit here, is the idea that to find your style you must first find, or know, yourself.

Individualism, the aggrandizement of the one as distinct from the many, is surely the root of style as we interpret the word today. Our heroes and heroines, as necessary to a cult of individualism as are saints to organized religion, are the larger-than-life personalities, capable of big, careless gestures—extravagant, courageous, generous.

Given the niggling erosion in our daily lives of the personal factor, fed as we are like sausagemeat through sophisticated technology, it is perhaps hardly surprising that people feel vulnerable, specks of grain trapped between millstones which might at any moment grind exceeding small. Too familiar to be a panic situation, it is still the background against which our lives are lived. Individualism in this context—any reassuring evidence that the lone individual can generate enough self-belief, humour, talent, originality or cheek to challenge the system and stand out from the crowd—reminds us that *homo sapiens* is still at once wiser and less predictable than market research studies would allow. It is pounced upon with delighted relief, shading off—when the challenge is particularly outrageous—into grumbling tolerance. Style is now one of the defensive weapons the individual resorts to in an ambiguous world.

However much we are intrigued or entertained, by the 'form and manner' aspects of contemporary style, it is, I think, for a content the dictionary ignores—its fundamentally positive attitude to life, its cheeky whistling in the dark, its exaltation of individual as against crowd values—that we observe, nurture and cherish its wildly disparate manifestations today.

Style and interior design or, more pragmatically, what people do to make their homes more interesting, attractive, comfortable, are inseparably linked. Putting one's home together is everyman's opportunity to be visually creative.

People have always cared about the appearance and amenity of their homes. Domesticity is a plant which thrives in favourable conditions. But I doubt if there has ever been a time when so many people lavished so much time, thought, money, and care on their domiciles, whether these be basement flats, terrace houses or run-down mansions.

Seminal Rooms

Anyone in possession of those freakishly sensitive antennae which pick up on trends and styles while they are still gestating, will have experienced the surprise of finding that a whim or fancy that seemed entirely private and spontaneous, was simultaneously occurring to hundreds, perhaps thousands, of other people. In fashion this happens all the time. Designers produce their new shape, and the shape is so ubiquitous it looks as though they must have worked in collaboration. Fashion-conscious individuals are prompted, out of the blue, to knit sweaters from string, say, or cut their trousers off at mid-calf and, looking about them, are astonished to see that every other fashion-conscious individual is wearing string sweaters and cropped pants. Is this the collective unconscious at work or further, sobering proof that there is nothing new under the sun?

Something analogous happens with the inspiration for room decor. Suddenly—it feels sudden in retrospect, though such complex happenings are usually gradual and fitful—a particular style of interior, historical or contemporary, begins to exert a mysterious fascination, stirring the imaginations of people who don't know each other and probably imagine, if they stop to think about it, that they are alone in their enthusiasm. My own first excited hunch about Early American interiors grew from such random, disconnected information that there was no reason to suppose that anyone else was interested. The difficulty in obtaining research material made it seem even less likely. But, of course, just as I pounced excitedly on the first available full-colour photos of these primly hospitable interiors, with their warm but muted colours and stiffly charming use of stencilled decoration, the Early American Style was a long way past a twinkle in a designer's eye. Lynn le Grice was working out her first stencil kit, exhibitions of Early Americana were being mounted, people were hanging patchwork quilts on their walls or stencilling borders on their painted floors, and what felt to me like a lonely passion was already a collective love affair. The lifespan of one of these trends is perhaps ten years, which is about the time it has taken for the Early American craze to take off in every direction and become so universally accepted that a glossy magazine feels confident enough to offer stencilled wooden chests to their readers for a special price of £200 (when you and I *know* that we could pick up an old blanket box in a saleroom and give it the Early American treatment for £15 or so).

Seminal rooms may be comparatively recent ones, like the all-white rooms designed by Syrie Maugham, decorator wife of the writer Somerset

John Soane was a master of surprise and inventive exploitation of space. Adding a stone balcony to the front of his London drawing-room, changed existing windows into openings—note bookcases slotted into old shutter spaces—leading to light-filled space beyond. Dark skirting ties in with the floor, while an ornamental fillet defines new areas of interest on the walls.

11

The bland elegance of Syrie Maugham's white-on-white treatment could be imposed on rooms of most shapes, sizes and periods to create the effect of sophisticated relaxation, of laid-back glamour, which went with the age of cocktails, cruises and frothy Hollywood comedies. Texture, as in the sculpted pile, white-on-white rugs made for her by Marion Dorn, was a subtle but necessary element in the overall look, which was never—as later all-white architects' rooms tended to be—clinical or austere. Colour, in the form of paintings, flowers, walls of books, is noticeably absent from most shots of rooms of the Thirties, as is clutter. Maybe the prevailing neutrality, impersonality even, had something to do with the affluent maintaining a low profile in times of financial insecurity and increasing unemployment, as well as displaying a fashionable acquaintance with the stark dictates of modernism.

Maugham. These startled her coevals in the Thirties, but now look yawningly familiar, prototypes of so many of today's glamorously null interiors from Park Lane penthouse to Arab bank. More often, though, as with the Early American influence, they are largely forgotten historical antecedents which a mysterious conjunction of taste and need rediscovers with sharpened appetite. Today's seminal rooms would include such influences as the Shakers, Sir John Soane, eccentric architect of the Bank of England, Biedermeyer, the Baroque, Claude Monet, Mies van der Rohe, and the English designer of the Twenties and Thirties, Eileen Gray. An indigestible pudding of styles lumped together but, of course, no intelligent contemporary would dream of throwing together a bit of each like a cocktail and producing the dream decor. Influences combine more subtly, so that this room awakens new feelings about colour, that one a hunger for radical simplicity, yet another an appreciation of architectural games; and what emerges from the slow simmering of such disparate elements is a synthesis, a new flavour out of known ingredients. If current interior design seems uncertain which way to go, like its parent discipline, architecture, it may be because the mix of influences is unprecedentedly rich. When the avant-garde of a century ago, men like Rossetti, Whistler, Arthur Lazenby Liberty (founder of the store of that name) discovered Japanese style, its studied and refined simplicity appealed in the context of Victorian overcrowding, its promiscuity of taste.

Against a background of fringed plush, buttoned loveseats, whatnots stuffed with knick-knacks and gaudy Berlin wool-work, the aesthetes' cult of uncluttered rooms, gently washed in clear pale colours, set out with a few elegant pieces and a collection of Japanese prints, must have had considerable shock value. Oscar Wilde's white, yellow and black drawing-room (Wilde lectured in America on interior decoration) was almost as much a badge of aestheticism as the green carnation sported by the dandy in W. S. Gilbert's witty light opera, *Patience*.

> You may rank as an apostle in the high aesthetic band
> If you walk down Piccadilly with a poppy or a lily in your medieval hand.

Seminal rooms set trends and influence interiors but they finally transcend fashion. What they exemplify, as a rule, is a style played out to its limits, coherent, fixed for all time. This style can be the whipcord purity of line in the furnishings of New England Shaker rooms, the dazzling rococo ebullience of the royal hunting lodge built for Empress Amalia, named the Amalienburg after her, or the tough modern chic of Eileen Gray's seaside villa at Roquebrune, where clichés of today's high tech style, such as studded rubber flooring and tubular handrails are played off against her own luxurious furniture designs in glass and steel, or impeccable lacquer. Another seminal room of our times, combining a painter's eye for colour with a fresh approach to traditional bourgeois furnishing, must be Claude Monet's wonderful dining-room at Giverny, where almost everything from curvaceous armoires to rush-seated chairs is painted in two tones of yellow as foil to blue and white porcelain, Japanese prints and floor of chequered terracotta tiles.

Significantly, seminal rooms are almost always the work of one creative yet intensely practical mind, overseeing everything from the overall first conception to the final placing of the light switches. This gives them extraordinary integrity even where they have been transplanted to museums —like Whistler's exquisite Peacock Room in Washington's Smithsonian Institute—and shorn of their original furnishings.

The nearer a seminal room gets to a 'formula', a clever decorating look with easily recognizable elements, the more immediately influential it becomes and the more widely copied. Syrie Maugham's trademarks, chrome and mirror screens, pale lacquer, scroll-shaped occasional tables, subtly varied

'Strange ornaments [are] to be seen in the houses of very charming people … wax flowers, horrible things perpetrated in Berlin wool, endless antemacassars … which seem to reduce life to the level of an eternal washing day.'

OSCAR WILDE

Painters' homes are invariably rewarding, intensely personal and vivid, though not always as irresistible in colouring and style as Claude Monet's much-loved and lived-in house at Giverny. Who but a French artist of genius would have contemplated painting such dignified traditional armoires two tones of yellow to merge with his dining-room scheme and set off both the blue and white porcelain and subtly-coloured Japanese prints? Who but Monet would have determined that his dining-room revel in all the sensuous delights—colour, form and texture as well as the bourgeois comforts of good food and drink and large sturdy chairs round a capacious table?

shades and textures of white-on-white, added up to a sophisticated yet impersonal decor which could be—and was, for it had an immediate success—imposed on any large, featureless room. Such bland elegance seems not to date, and the world is still full of 'all white' look-alikes.

Architectural students wander reverently through Sir John Soane's house—now a museum—in Lincoln's Inn Fields, decorators and dealers enthuse over Biedermeyer chairs and Eileen Gray rugs, and almost everyone is moved by the austere grace of a Shaker interior. Latterly, with neo-classical motifs returning to favour, the Palladian interior, with its architectonic use of fresco-painted scenes, *trompe-l'oeil* columns, niches and statues, and squares and lozenges of boldly painted 'marble', has become a prime source of inspiration. Ladies who have never heard of Palladio are mad about murals and marbling and wall colours as subtly time worn as those of a Renaissance palazzo. It has even become profitable for the more adventurous of today's small army of young decorative painters to spend time in Italy or Brussels learning the techniques of painting in fresco, a labour-intensive ancient method of laying colours into wet lime plaster which proceeds at approximately the rate of one square yard per day, and remains the most durable and sympathetic wall surface ever invented.

Most of the rooms I have been discussing, much photographed, visited and argued about, are part of the public domain of style. But we all have our own seminal rooms remembered from childhood, fleetingly visited or maybe just down the road. My own would include a tiny upstairs room in the C'a Rezzonico in Venice with Tiepolo frescos of masked carnival figures in lovely, limpid colours against a scheme of nun-like grey and white simplicity. Another would be Vita Sackville-West's tower room at Sissinghurst in Kent, stone walls lined with books, a scholar's retreat. Then there was a panelled chamber at Blois, in France, almost bare of furniture, but painted such a delicate in-between colour of green and grey and blue that the place had the tender clarity of a Vermeer. More robust in tone with its freestyle painted 'graining' set off by pilasters and mouldings in green-blue, was one of my favourite Early American interiors, a plain but comely panelled parlour with polished plank floor, brick hearth and little low doors and beamed ceiling. Old, a little odd, more sturdy than grand, what affected me about these rooms was a feel rather than a look, the quality Mario Praz identifies in his classic book on European decoration as '*stimmung*', a German word meaning roughly 'intimate mood'. I could have drawn a chair up to the desk or table and started living in any of them—indeed they seemed to have anticipated my arrival.

I have never set out to copy any one of them, though in-between blues and rich reds tend to appear wherever I live. But the *stimmung*, yes, I do attempt to recreate, drawing on memories which have become second nature, a fondness for books, pools of lamplight, crowded corners, layers of rugs, friendly furniture, fireplaces with, at least now and then, a fire. One day I might get round to painting a ceiling *après* Tiepolo, though probably not in fresco. The rooms important to one's developing style are not usually the ones full of clever ideas to purloin, but the ones which make you feel, as you enter them, at home, at ease, the right human size. There may be nice touches—though I remember only red cupboards in blue rooms and Tiepolo's delectable marbled insets like *petits fours*—but it is the totality of the room one surrenders to. In different ways and varying degrees all seminal rooms, public or private, give off a strong sense of belonging, which I suppose is close to the idea of *genius loci*. Unlike the rooms which disappear from consciousness when you walk out of them or switch off the light, these reassure because we sense that they go on independently existing, with a rich, secret life of their own after we have left them.

Opposite page: The Breakfast Room, from the Soane Museum, is another example of Soane's original way of reordering interior spaces and introducing light from unexpected sources, here the small glazed octagonal dome above, a circular theme developed in the round mirrored insets round the curved ceiling. Typically Soanian is the placing of a narrow cabinet to exactly balance an existing door. Few homes exhibit such intensely pondered, or meticulously crafted, detail. Soane spent a fortune creating what amounts to a gigantic 'cabinet of curiosities' to house his collections of classical statuary, coins, books, and became involved in a lawsuit with his family when they discovered his plan to bequeath the building and contents to the nation, as a museum. Their loss was our gain—the mind boggles at the thought of what full-blown Victorian taste would have done to Soane's astonishing, highly idiosyncratic masterpiece.

'The design and decoration of this limited space present a succession of those fanciful effects which constitute the poetry of architecture.'
JOHN SOANE

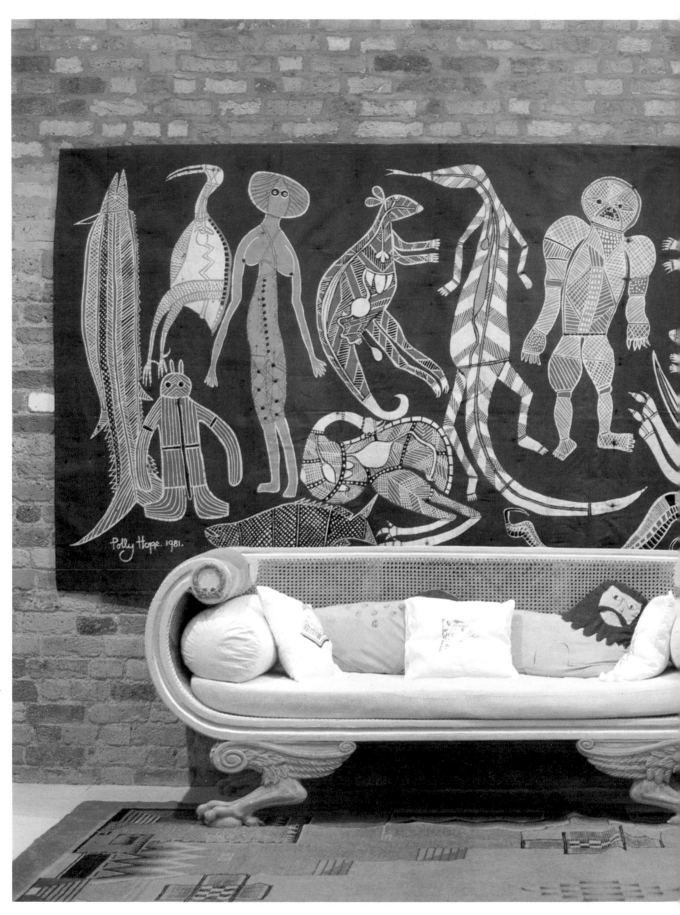

Designer Style

Those who have a working connection with the inside of houses—designers, decorators, dealers in antique or modern furniture—tend to think of their own homes as showplaces, pudding proof of how their special talents work out under the most favourable circumstances. Obviously, it helps the image if the home base is seen by visitors to function superbly and look wonderful. It is hard to remember how many decorators have been launched by word-of-mouth publicity, by those invaluable, influential ladies who make a fetish of being up-to-the-minute and telling their friends about this brilliant person they met who does incredible rooms with brown paper and hessian. Be that as it may, home for these people is not just where they hang their hat—it is shop window, often in the case of dealers, shop extension, where interesting but hard-to-sell pieces can be shown off to their best advantage, tricked out with carefully chosen knick-knacks and flowers. One successful dealer/decorator (the boundaries between these activities tend to blur) I know has the disconcerting habit of intercepting admiring glances and whispering across the dinner table, 'Of course, you know everything here is on the line, dear!' In other words, up for sale if you can agree on a price.

The pressure to make a production number of one's pad, be it city basement or rural Gothic villa, in most cases enforces perfectionist standards. You would be correct in assuming, therefore, that these are not places where normal domestic sloppiness is allowed to encroach. Prams in the hall, unmade beds, unplumped cushions, wilting flower arrangements, chipped sinks full of unwashed crockery—no way. There are exceptions, dealers extraordinary who have elevated the shabby grand, the nonchalant swank of splendid old things with all their scars and patches showing, into a personal aesthetic but they only go to prove that breaking the rules needs great confidence, panache, and a mischievously subtle sense of style.

More often, the pro's home errs on the side of self-conscious, parade-ground smartness. Nervous guests wonder if they dare stub out a cigarette in one of those exquisite Chinese dishes or safely rest a glass on the dazzling patina of a piecrust-edged mahogany occasional table, not to mention the possible grime one's boots might deposit on the oyster linen velvet upholstery. Having brazened out these small problems, there is invariably much to look at and admire. We are, after all, talking about technical experts in the field, who have made their reputations polishing up their clients' taste and helping their domestic arrangements to work more smoothly. I never visit one of these

Take an extraordinary bateau-shaped sofa squatting on huge claw feet, stand it on a Thirties rug in front of an exposed brick wall featuring an ebullient wall hanging of Australian aboriginal life, animal and human, and you have a bold and brilliant encapsulation of style. The style is all Polly Hope's, and being the versatile artist/designer/sculptress that she is, she makes connections the rest of us might not think of, rubbing the sophisticated up against primitive.

Low-key colouring, emphasis on architectural bone structure, florals, fabrics and femininity banished in favour of line and shape, every piece a classic of its time—this epitomizes the designer approach to rooms. One carefully positioned picture, one ditto pot, are the only purely ornamental objects allowed to encroach upon a room where everything else observes the rule that form follows function. Eclecticism is part of the game for those who can afford exemplary antiques, but it always stays this side of collectomania—no tat, no frippery, no junk and, heavens above, no kitsch.

places without taking copious mental notes on colours, unexpected combinations, even the smallest details like the sorts of mounts and frames they choose for old prints.

Of the three groups, designers (who are often architecturally trained) are the theorists—everything in a designer's home is making a statement. A strongly contemporary look is mandatory though the results—given the current battle of styles between high tech, post-modern, ornamentalist—can look oddly different. In all of them, however, you will find the emphasis on structure, space, light, making for a certain hard-edged austerity. Clutter is out, banished to expensive custom-built storage units; furniture—what there is of it—is chosen for sculptural line, rather than comfort; no scatter cushions or festoon blinds and not a chintz to be seen.

Older, richer designers favour an eclectic mix of classics of all periods—an Eames chair, a Thonet bentwood rocking chair, a Windsor stick back. Sturdy provincial pieces in well-polished wood are permissible: Jacobean carved oak chests, French Provençal armoires, an Italian credenza. They tend to shy away from colour, too. The look is all white apart from a few chaste contemporary prints, the obligatory geometric kelim rug. All these things are expensive, so younger designers have to impress in other ways. They go for colour in a big way. They like the clash of vivid red, blue, green, yellow, preferably in shiny plastic, laminates, lacquer, tiles aligned as precisely as graph paper. Their living spaces are cheerless, but their bathrooms and kitchens are expensive, functional, stunning and highly influential. Post-modernists also say it with colour, but not wishing to be confused with high technicians, they favour weird pastels, chilly ice blue, mauve pink, lots of grey and the story is in the finish—marbled, stippled in a blizzard of coloured dots or graduated from light to dark like Thirties cinemas and powder rooms.

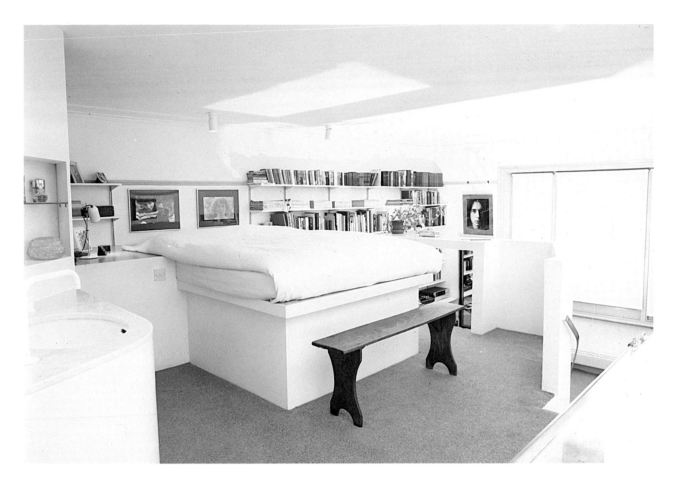

High-tech furnishings lean towards canvas and stainless steel, with unobtrusive unit or built-in seating, but post-modern is allowed to be kitsch, camp and a trifle sinister—monster-sized, Odeon-style three-piece suites covered in scratchy uncut moquette, Thirties tub chairs in early fake hide, standing either side of a small table, junk chairs shrouded in white sheeting or canvas. Post-modernists and ornamentalists put all their ideas and energy into making something surrealist, a touch grandiose, of their public spaces while their bedrooms usually look depressed, and kitchen and bathrooms are often casually squalid.

Where professional designers often score is on organization of storage, sophisticated lighting systems and inventive re-thinking of cheap modern materials. Their best kitchens and bathrooms are meticulously planned to combine maximum use of space with least possible upkeep. Be warned, though, high design in any area of domestic life comes expensive, demanding good materials and excellent workmanship to underpin its slick appearance and impressive performance. 'Less is more' was the celebrated battle cry of the whole modernist movement whose heroes and heroines, like Le Corbusier, Aalto and Eileen Gray still affect the shape of things to come. But less widely bruited is the interesting and ironic fact that their less was a good deal more in the crude cash sense. The famous Barcelona Pavilion was made of travertine, grey glass and green marble; Aalto's chairs used stainless steel not chrome; Eileen Gray exploited the dandified combination of bone simple modern shapes with sumptuous, costly Chinese lacquer; and, today, bright interpreters like Eva Jiricna make use of expensive finishing and spraying techniques to give their gutsy industrial-type components the necessary class.

With interior decorators we move, broadly speaking, into another time warp. Vital components of the decorator style are lavish upholstery, fabrics,

The upstairs of the downstairs on the opposite page, this ingeniously contrived master bedroom and bathroom on a balcony (not a large balcony, either) takes the uncompromising designer look even further towards functional purity— white everywhere from walls to duvet to washbasin, monkish grey for the carpet against which a sliver of polished wood bench glows like the sculptural object it also is. Unlike most bedrooms there is nothing random to fall over, such space as there is, is carefully kept clear, which gives a soothing sense of calm. Too comfortable to be ascetic, the reduction to essentials of this approach to living does have something anchoritish about it, more contemplative than a mere machine for living.

19

'Finally, the whole room or apartment becomes a mould of the spirit, the case without which the soul would feel like a snail without its shell.'
MARIO PRAZ

colour schemes, comfort, prettiness and, if they are good at their job, atmosphere. The best interior decorating work done today comes about when a client of positive ideas, style and money meets up with a decorator with the nerve to argue, and the sense and skill to interpret. Most clients, however, only know what they *don't* like and from this negative situation what emerges is safe, expensive and boring. In their own homes interior decorators, glutted on the rich fare their clients demand, often go for an artfully casual innocence— sprigged muslin rather than bolts of chintz, colour-washed walls rather than hand-blocked wallpaper, crunchy reed matting rather than pile carpet, faded gilt rather than pompous ormolu. But this deliberately 'poor' look is deceptive. Look closely at a decorator's home and you will notice a lavish attention to detail—the lampshades custom-made of pleated linen; hand-painted paper; the charming bird or flower prints lining the staircase walls are mounted and framed so sensitively they blend as sweetly as the colours of a faded quilt; the cushions are filled with down and their loose covers (albeit of humble materials like denim, linen) fit as precisely as a Savile Row suit.

Any successful decorator has his own list of skilled people who restore, paint furniture, re-gild, lacquer, make lampshades, upholster, frame pictures, run up the most elaborate curtains and covers, repair old textiles, rugs and reproduce existing plasterwork, mouldings or metalwork. They daily see, compare and handle a wide range of textiles, trimmings, wallpapers, borders, paint colours and finishes. It is part of their job to be ahead with current trends in interiors and to know where to go for anything from door handles to four-poster beds. From this multiplicity of choice, the best evolve their own style as recognizable to clients as, say, the discreet sexiness of Jean Muir dresses or the sophisticated bravura of Oscar de la Renta. British decorators are famous for their skill at combining cosiness with an upper-class sort of style, the 'country house' look established under Queen Victoria (squashy chairs in pretty floral slip covers creating oases of comfort amid the sterner lines of antique furnishings) and subtly updated from time to time ever since. In their own homes British decorators tend to create a cottage-scaled version of the same look, charming, comfortable, gentle in colour, masses of flowers, pictures, knick-knacks and a careful avoidance of the brashly modern, kitchen and bathrooms excepted. It is a feminine friendly look, whether practised by

This could only be an antique dealer's room, fairly revelling in the quiddity, the thinginess of things—an outrageously lush floral carpet, a long way après *Aubusson, a captivatingly ruched though slightly dilapidated chair strewn with a pot pourri of faded needlework, the warm gleam of old lacquer, a frisky group of brass ornaments on the mantelpiece. Because the dealer in question is a woman, and beautiful, the room has an overflowing warmth of colour and texture, as well as an abundance of cherished things. There is the confidence of a 'good eye' behind the knowledge that things noble and things whacky can be on good terms with each other if held together visually in rich but melting colours. There is common sense, too, in the decision that if you have to use cheap lining cotton for curtains let there be yards and yards of it.*

men or women and a world away from the awesomely grand effects in the modern idiom created by the French François Catroux or the lavish over-the-top extravaganzas of that other international jet-set darling, Italian Renzo Mongiardino. Just how divergent decorating styles can be is startlingly displayed at Daylesford, once a conventional country house with typically restrained decor, recently re-done by Mongiardino for the von Thyssen family, with crimson Genoese cut velvet on the saloon walls, hundreds of yards of padded paisley print lining the corridors and stair wells, hand-painted friezes, walls hand painted to suggest stamped leather.

If line is a designer fetish and fabric and finish a decorator one, the dealer is overboard about *things*: choice old pieces, eccentric newer ones, cushions, pictures, prints, bric-à-brac, irresistible oddities crammed together hugger-mugger. Dealers' homes are notable for atmosphere, a sort of thickening and flavouring of the air which derives quite simply from the powerful presences of so many things. The effect can be spooky *à la* Miss Havisham, sentimental and fussy as a Victorian valentine, or weirdly sophisticated when the dealer is into retro or deco or art nouveau. It is hard not to envy dealers their constant access to rare and beautiful objects. How much easier to make a place look good with the help of a lacquered cabinet, armfuls of faded needlework cushions, or a set of darkly powerful Jacobean portraits! And what about all those delicious bits of nonsense—beaded pincushions, Staffordshire figures, wisps of old lace, bouquets of wax flowers or peacock feathers, which look so much more adorable massed together (as every stallholder knows) in gypsyish confusion. But remind yourself that most of the desirable objects in a dealer's home are transients and that what you are admiring has the impermanence of a stage set. Dealers are always falling for something or other, a passion for acquisition being what makes them tick, but the temptation to hang on to something special has always to be balanced against making a living.

Only the grandest dealers can afford to specialize, limiting themselves to an historical period or one type of object—old clocks, desks, lamps. Any dealer with a 'good eye', however, seeks out things with personal appeal and is always rediscovering the charms of neglected or unfashionable lines—bamboo furniture one year, deco fittings another—and buying them up cheaply with the idea of promoting them and making a decent profit.

'You may be sure that any decoration is futile . . . when it does not remind you of something beyond itself, of something of which it is but a visible symbol.'

WILLIAM MORRIS

Grand Style

Kings, the powerful and the very rich have never been in any doubt that where and how you live is a potent reminder to an envious world of what a formidable personage you are. An occasional philosopher-king figure, the Emperor Augustus or Thomas Jefferson, may have elected to live austerely and impress with other means. For the most part, though, rulers and the wealthy from Nero to the Rothschilds have greedily availed themselves of all the worldly goods and gewgaws which the Bible warns make it harder for them to enter Heaven than for a camel to pass through a needle's eye—gold, jewels, marble, rich rugs and embroideries, mechanical marvels like clockwork singing birds or ceilings that open to sift rose petals on to the guests beneath. All the marvels recounted in children's fairy tales have been commanded to exist at some time or other by men and women so powerful, wilful and dangerous that to look baffled or act dumb (or indeed anything but eager, enthusiastic and competent), was tantamount to suicide. At this extravagant level, the grand style was consciously intended not merely to impress, but to strike awe and fear into lesser beings, from ambassadors to serving wenches. Unrestrained, it easily burgeons into megalomania and the nightmarish extravagance and frigidity of palaces like those of Philip II of Spain, mad King Ludwig of Bavaria, or (to my mind) the Sun King at Versailles. Spectacular, but, perhaps mercifully, intolerable to average people.

Descending several notches socially, to the level of mere nobles or millionaires, one still finds the urge to dazzle and impress but usually tempered by common sense and domestic life. Think of Bess of Hardwick's immense glazed mullioned windows at a time when glass was prohibitively costly. More generally one finds a conscious display of the most expensive dyes and paint colours as well as the usual profusion of treasures. But the peculiar charm of the English grand style, as exemplified in the many still surviving stately homes, is that it wore a human, domestic face at least outside those parading rooms designed for show and spectacle. As a nation, it seems, we are uncomfortable with heroic gestures and our true genius finds its expression in settings which promise comfort and intimacy, like studies, private sitting-rooms and nurseries; or proclaim their purpose, like those wonderful galleries (for indoor walking on wet days) in Tudor and Jacobean houses; or occasionally, even kitchens—isn't the breathtaking kitchen in the Brighton Pavilion with its palm tree pillars, exposed brick walls hung with copper utensils, even more of a draw than its lavish public apartments?

No British Royal ever got more heavily into debt, or exhibited a more cultivated style in so doing than the endearingly feckless Prince Regent in the decoration of his fantastic seaside palace, the Brighton Pavilion. The Music Room is its masterpiece. Forty-four skilled craftsmen worked for two years to complete a dazzling oriental fairytale setting in carmine, gold and silver (which left Prinny's contemporaries, even his own Mrs Fitzherbert, at a loss for words).

There's a nonchalant charm to this much lived-in bedroom, the owner's favourite retreat—spilling over with books, papers, treasures, casual swags of old lace. Though unmistakably feminine, it is bold in its liking for striking pieces, big pictures, un-bedroom colours, the bizarre ornament. Mellow, singular, this room is a romantic version of shabby grand.

Opposite page: There is more period consistency in this example of grand-ness in miniature (a London flat) than one usually finds, which is because the owner, Cornelia Bailey, has an uncompromising fondness for good Empire furniture of the severely tailored sort, embellished with a little gilding. Unusually, for a professional fabric restorer, her taste is towards polished wood rather than beautiful decaying textiles, and her way of setting them off is to pick one good strong colour and stick to it for walls, curtains and some of the furnishings.

British grand style as it survives today—chopped about, mongrelized, but still flourishing in pockets—is something we pride ourselves upon, not for its unabashed luxury, but for the much more ambiguous reason that we, or the decorators representing us, can contrive a look which is grand—without apparent striving. Any decorator, so our insular reasoning runs, can contrive a grand, rich, impressive effect on a lavish budget, by choosing only fine antiques, expensive fabrics and materials, good pictures. The trouble with this sort of scenario is that you can read it at a glance, and all you see is price tags. Only royalty, with their own glamour, can get away with it. The shabby-grand aesthetic revolves around the discovery that age and down-at-heelness give distinguished objects and rooms a poetic patina, an allure infinitely more poignant than they ever had in their green youth. This sensibility comes naturally to a country whose ancestral homes—till lately—were wonderfully, unselfconsciously threadbare, shadowy with dust and scented with dry rot. Anyone can be forgiven for thinking, on entering a shabby grand interior—peopled with strangely ghostly chairs and rugs, paintings too dark to see, mirrors too stained and pewtery to reflect, curtains in tatters and cushions oozing out of their covers—that they have stumbled into an over-sized hovel, which a good dusting and polishing and a few hours with needle and thread would do much to improve. But, given the smallest streak of suggestibility, they cannot fail to thrill to the information—casually stumbled upon—that these same greyish needleworked chairs that the dogs sprawl on so familiarly, are three hundred years old and in their original covers worked, or so one conjectures, by one of those lashless dames staring through layers of varnish and grime from the ancestral portraits. How nonchalantly aristocratic, how cool, to take all this priceless, decaying loot for granted, gossiping about a neighbour's open day or arguing about the gardener's boy, while the dry rot

spreads inexorably and the dogs thoughtfully chew another tassel off a Jacobean *petit-point* cushion.

Something like this admiring *frisson* animates the many contemporary recreations of shabby grandeur though in these updated versions convenience is not forgotten and comfortable chairs and sofas, in quiet shapes and colours, are allowed to mingle with tattered bergère chairs, or straight-backed Jacobean settles. What is not old—because it was put together last month—like the wall coverings or curtain fabrics is chosen to look as if it were. Wall finishes of great subtlety, loosely marbled, water-coloured on to gesso to give the gently discoloured bloom of Italian fresco, delicately striated or mottled with rags, are preferred to wallpaper, bare polished boards piled with layers of rugs worn almost to transparency are preferred to fitted carpets. Curtains might be saleroom treasures, complete with original hand-knotted fringes, tassels and tiebacks, or hand-blocked in colours which mimic decades of fading and use or, failing these, one of the currently fashionable revivals, the so-called document chintzes based on surviving eighteenth- and nineteenth-century designs. Seating may be arranged in conversational groups, but other furniture (if it isn't antique, forget it here) tends to stand in its traditionally allotted place (console and pier glass between windows, sofa table behind a sofa). There is a liking for symmetry—pairs of huge Chinese porcelain jars or busts standing on pedestals, two girandole mirrors—because this gives a grand effect. Upholstered stools are preferred to coffee tables. Fireplaces are kept immaculately swept, logs neatly arranged ready to set ablaze, their garnish of tongs, poker and fender usually of polished steel rather than brass. Chairs to flop into, as opposed to the precious variety, are loose covered to look like old-fashioned dust covers in pinstriped shirting cotton. The chandelier aloft is for effect really, since the room is invariably lit by table lamps supplemented by a few picture lights over the really good paintings. One or two beautifully arranged vases of flowers, or hot-house plants such as cyclamen or azaleas, but no riots of greenery. Current reading, books and magazines, is allowed to accumulate on the fireside stool or Pembroke table, but bookcases are usually absent from these rooms, banished to a study or—in ultra-grand contexts—library.

Many more people covet the off-handedly grand look than could conceivably afford it in its undiluted state. There simply are not enough girandoles, chandeliers, Chinese jars or needleworked sofas to go round and they change hands at Sotheby's and Christie's for small fortunes. Two or three fine things are essential to fix the style as shabby grand rather than shabby genteel but, having said that, it is surprising how effectively the right atmosphere can be conjured up around them if the person concerned knows what they are aiming for. Fairly spacious rooms are the basic requirement, difficult in cities, but by no means impossible in the Scottish Highlands (many people are buying run-down castles) or the remoter counties well outside the commuter belts. These white elephants (often neatly quartered, and sold off as manageable segments of the grand tradition) must have hung on to their grand features (marble fireplaces, flagged floors, fancy cornices, solid panelled doors) but unattractive accretions like exposed pipes and vast radiators ridged like concertinas are tolerated if they are old and unabashed.

What shabby-grand fanciers invoke to fill these aching spaces in lieu of the correct props, is a good deal of artistic licence, in the way of fantastic murals, *trompe l'oeil*, marbling, graining and sky-painted ceilings with clouds. Stencils too, so long as these are applied so artfully that they resemble old and precious embroidery, rather than the cheery hearts and flowers decorations which go with the cottage style. Luxurious pretend finishes like these 'finish off' a bleakly bare room with a suitable swagger, obviating the need for Old Masters, tapestries and real statues in niches. Floors are not usually such a

'I cannot help suspecting that the more elegance, the less virtue, in all times and countries.'

U.S. PRESIDENT JOHN ADAMS

'Our tastes greatly alter. The lad does not care for the child's rattle, and the old man does not care for the young man's whore.'

SAMUEL JOHNSON

problem. Stone flags, cleaned up and polished, always look noble, decent boards ditto, while really grotty ones can be painted and disguised with a scatter of rugs.

The imposingly overscaled pieces suited to big rooms are still often much cheaper in the country, so local auction rooms, local dealers and jumble sales are good sources for shabby grand interiors. Probably the hardest part of contriving the look is finding necessary etceteras like lamps, small tables and hall chairs with a pedigree look at mongrel prices. One answer is to become a dealer, ferrying fashionable tat to the big cities and buying one or two properly constituted items with the profits. Another is to bone up on restoration techniques, like invisible china mending or gilding or delicate joinery. Then snap up all the overpainted mirrors, lame chairs and tables, and chipped or cracked pots and jars—anything which has the look at an affordable price. With dealers growing so canny and ubiquitous, there is much more competition even in the 'slightly faulty' department, but it is still possible to discover decaying gems in country barns, or in the trash section of local salerooms, or even by studying cards in tobacconists' windows, where country people often advertise things for sale. In time you develop an instinct for reading around the bare and often misleading descriptions. 'Antique' usually isn't, whereas 'old' well may be, albeit hideously overpainted or missing splats or legs or with the springs dropping out. All this takes time, no doubt, but that is a commodity still to be found in country life, at least on long dark winter evenings, which is when people ambitious to feather their grand nests can stitch lampshades, cane seats, mend china and learn the crafts of gessoing and water gilding, patching veneers and marquetry. Such is the obsessive excitement of restoring formerly fine old buildings to their proper state that a surprising number of people really do set themselves to master a range of skills and become highly proficient at them. How many of the country ladies now offering to handpaint china 'blanks' to match the wallpaper, started out doing a little invisible mending on the side?

Above left: Architect Nigel Coates and his eccentrically lofty London home might have been designed for each other. Neither is afraid of going over the top, the tiny hall/dining-room swanking in two gigantic portico doorways, Nigel unhesitatingly capitalizing on this bonus by marbling them both in a dark and moody palette of blues and black, with touches of gold wax rubbed on with the fingers. Note the Soanian mirror inset jokily let into the table, and further reflective aids in perky driving mirrors—'like exclamation marks'—propped in each corner.

Above right: One stylish solution to the room (through the portico) which seems to go on up for ever is to take it further still, with elongated flower arrangements, ladder-like prints and a grandiose sky ceiling painted with blurry clouds. The effect here is deliberately artificial, surreal, it might be the set for a Gothic thriller set in a Viennese apartment block. A parody of the grand style, resolutely un-bourgeois.

Cottage Style

The standard definition of a cottage as a modest dwelling whose front door opens directly into the principal room (so, no hall, lobby or porch) is loose enough to include any vernacular building the world over, from South American adobe to Samoan longhouse. But, of course, cottage means something quite different to the British, a sentimentally idealized habitation, snuggling into a sunny pastoral setting under a bonnet of thatch, with roses wreathing the front door and clumps of hollyhocks and sweet-william either side. Such buildings do exist, their picturesqueness affectionately recorded by artists like Morland since the eighteenth century. Indeed the variety of vernacular building styles is an inexhaustibly interesting feature of the British landscape, whether one is thinking of the timbering and thatch of East Anglia, the mellow stone of the South West, or the stalwart crofts further north. Their look is one of having grown into their setting, be it snug village or lonely moor. But the cottage *idea*, the roses and thatch romanticism embroidered on tea cosies and tray cloths, is a quite recent phenomenon, projected on a receptive public by writers and artists in the late Victorian era and onwards. The most subconsciously affecting of them were perhaps the ones creating an imaginative world for children—Kate Greenaway, with her exquisitely costumed tinies sporting about a manicured village green, Beatrix Potter's animal characters bustling about lakeland pin-neat cottages of white-washed stone, even Arthur Rackham's darker visions of thatched cots under bare, black trees.

Cottage interiors, which were not formerly considered as picturesque as their exteriors—being in reality the dark, roughly furnished and primitive homes of impoverished agricultural labourers—were selectively re-invented in the process, to become the cosy heartland, all crooked and nooky, with a kettle steaming on the hob, brasses twinkling and floors scoured. The British imagination has yearned for them ever since. The cottage idea struck an immediate chord with the new class of house buyers spreading out, with the expansion of rail transport, round the fringes of large cities. To live in one's own little home, with one's own little garden and many picturesque cottagey touches like fake beams and inglenooks, plus improved plumbing and lighting, became the new suburban commuter's ideal. Glorified, it gave impetus to the garden city; debased by speculators, it created mile after mile of pebble-dashed conformity.

Given a sloped ceiling, a slice of oak beam, putting the cottage style together is a matter of keeping one's eyes open (quilt from market stall, lacy pillowcases in house sales, pretty knick-knacks at thrift shops) and not overdoing it. Real cottage style is modest, innocent—a friendly clutch of furnishings, crocheted cushion covers, old china of no special value or period, rather than a carefully co-ordinated decor planned down to the last lampshade. Colourful random quilts, a stool for the bedside table, a jolly red lamp, lingerie pillows add up here to an effect of great charm.

Cottage nostalgia took a new turn after World War II. Instead of preferring new houses with cottagey touches, people began to search out real, rough, unimproved old cottages and convert them into the adorable, cosy, idealized dwellings they felt they should be. A nice instance of nature copying art. Viewed at one level, the result of indiscriminate conversion has been a deplorable emasculation of countless authentic old buildings, their quirky interiors gutted and opened out to make room for more possessions. The good side, however, is that countless dwellings have been rescued from collapse and that, in recent years, thanks to the increased respect we are learning to feel towards old buildings in general, the new breed of cottagers is approaching their rural bolthole or retirement home with greater sensitivity as well as less spare cash.

Real cottages, by virtue of their smallness, oldness and oddities of construction have a powerful character of their own which tends to fight with

Jumble sale finds, unmatching chairs, flowers inside and out, a darkly glossy stone floor and a ceiling of massy oak beams add up to cottage atmosphere, a patchwork of effects which charms with its honesty. Little homes in the country are the most fun to furnish, their friendliness makes everything work and the occasional burst of gilded splendour looks all the more striking for its unpretentious setting.

The cottage nostalgia at the heart of the suburban dream could not find a more evocative expression than this appealing illustration by a pre-World War I artist of the tired commuter about to turn in at his own gate at the other side of which waits, silhouetted against the cosy glow inside, the devoted little wife. Cottaginess was as much a state of mind as a proliferation of fake rustic detail in tiled gables, leaded windows, crazy paving, inglenooks. It stood for peaceful domesticity in a setting healthier, both physically and morally, than the congested urban districts from which so many of the new suburban commuters originally came.

attempts to make them genteel, elegant or crisply modern. The most successfully stylish cottages observe this, going for folksy charm, colourfulness and plausibility. Patchwork quilts, rag rugs, rush mats, blue and white china, old prints, real fires, beat-up chairs and sofas draped in travelling rugs, scrubbed deal, geraniums on the windowsills and rush-seated stools are all part of this look. It is also hospitable to most authentic and vivid ethnic artefacts of a similarly peasant background, such as Indian embroideries or hand-painted peasant pottery. Alien, or so it seems to me, are such things as shaggy carpeting, fur rugs, twirly wrought iron, opulent upholstery or fabrics, contemporary prints in aluminium frames, chrome in any form, in fact anything too new, too chic, too flash or too self-conscious. Many people, charmed by the picturesque angles of attic bedrooms, are impelled at once towards Laura Ashley co-ordinated prints and papers, which seem suitably innocent, fresh and small scale. Indeed they are, but everything too matching, down to the frill on the festoon blinds, smothers the singularity of a cottage attic in unconvincing prettiness, when a gentle colour wash on the walls and ceiling, rugs on bare boards, frilly curtains and a couple of faded prints are all that it needs to underline its essential and touching rusticity. Cottage interiors, however small their windows and thick their storm defying walls, are constantly being tested by the natural world just outside, and this makes false notes doubly jarring. Retro kitsch, ingenious and amusing in an urban context, strikes a real bum note in the fens or wolds or dales.

Two variants on the cottage fantasy show how successfully this intrinsically modest flower can be transplanted. The first is the cottage *orné*, or glorified cottage, and the other the *rus in urbe* (country in the town) tradition.

The cottage *orné* was a sort of rural playhouse for eighteenth-century gentlemen (usually bachelors), a deliberately small-scale retreat where they could lead the simple life, commune with nature and recuperate from big city dissipations. Louis XV's Petit Trianon, where he and Madame de Pompadour escaped the pomp and intrigue of court life at Versailles, is one antecedent. Simple cotton hangings, and plain paintwork, set the innocent rustic mood at the Petit Trianon where, for diversion, the royal lover and his lady inspected the model farm instead of sauntering along formal gravelled *allées*, thick with courtiers and presided over by marble statuary. Vastly larger and more luxurious than real cottages, these charming residences were somewhat restrained in their interior style, refined rather than showy, though a playful dalliance with Gothic or chinoiserie influences was approved. The idea of the cottage *orné* has never ceased to attract artistic bachelors and, now that the supply of small but suitably distinguished buildings (gatehouses, lodges, old stables, follies) is almost exhausted, many small but less distinguished buildings, often in small country towns, are receiving the same treatment. The result, a modest little house giving no hint of the treasures within, has its own playfulness. Fine antiques, rugs, china, pictures, and *objets de vertu*, maybe a little more rustic than usual, are artfully disposed throughout small, prettily decorated rooms, to make the most of the contrast between simple setting and exquisite thing.

Strictly a converted barn but inclining, in its melange of rustic and sophisticated, towards the cottage orné *tradition, this country retreat has been inventively re-arranged and decorated by its owner, Diana Phipps. The kitchen opens straight out of the fake flagged great hall, round which a roped-off gallery leads to bed and bathrooms cleverly tucked, it seems, into the stone walls.*

This warm little snug of a room has been created by the simplest of means—woody graining in tinted scumble glaze on the wainscot, black lozenges painted on the plank floor, the most basic fireplace of exposed brick with a bolection moulding surround. Windsor chairs complete the effect of austere comfort—extra chairs are pegged up on the walls, New England style. A collection of earthy-coloured pottery and creamware, picked up in the local flea market, rounds out the overall mellowness and texture of this intensely atmospheric room.

Nothing better illustrates a deep cottage nostalgia than the way in which people living right in the centre of cities set out to create a countrified atmosphere, the comforting illusion that fields and not streets lie beyond their walls. A flourishing overgrown garden is the usual point of departure, but a slip of a balcony stuffed with pots and creepers will do if the interiors help the illusion along. Kitchens here set the style firmly, strongholds of stripped pine, scrubbed deal, baskets, pottery, windowsill herbs, moon-faced clocks, rush table mats, china jelly moulds, copper pots and pans. The feeling is of a generous cornucopia of natural goodies, great pyramids of shiny apples chosen for their looks as well as taste, cupboards and worktops (usually tiles) bursting with provender displayed in glass jars, stoneware pots or carefully collected antique biscuit tins. Good smells, like proving dough, apple tart and garlicky casseroles, go with this look. Jolly, generous, hospitable, it can topple into bohemian slapdashness, or a slightly twee rusticity, with corn dollies and dusty bundles of dried herbs. But it is a beneficent kitchen atmosphere notwithstanding, and some of the most memorable kitchens I know have been of this order.

The main rooms evoke rural atmosphere more suavely, with urban luxuries like central heating, music centres and huge colour tellies, artfully concealed so that your main impression is of a light, pretty, casual place, usually these days painted apricot or sky blue, with maybe a stencilled border or flourish somewhere, and lots of cushiony, flowery, wicker chairs or loose-covered easy chairs. Curtains, table covers, loose covers, tend to be chintzy, at least floral; the floor may well be covered in matting and a few rugs. Family mementoes are strewn throughout the knick-knacks, which might include a collection of hand-painted china displayed in a corner cupboard. Lots of flowers, including some dried ones, plants, large open bowls of pot pourri enriching the scent of the almost obligatory open fire burning real logs delivered after dark by a new breed of urban entrepreneurs who make a decent living supplying fuel to sentimental romantics living in smokeless zones. Dozing over a glass of port by the leaping fire, one might well be in—not a real cottage, with its draughts and other occasional harsh reminders of the struggle involved in creating comfort in a rudely natural context—but in the super cottage, sweet smelling, warm and homely, which is as much a part of the national mythology as maypoles, harvest festivals, home-made elderberry wine and Sussex Pond Pudding.

'(Strawberry Hill) is a little plaything house that I got out of Mrs Chenevix's shop, and is the prettiest bauble you ever saw. It is set in enamelled meadows, with filigree hedges.'

HORACE WALPOLE

33

The Hope studio/des. res. again, showing the balcony arrangement at one end which takes desk, bed and a sofa or two, plus a ragged frieze of green plants. Aside from boarding in the roof, cleaning off the brick walls and putting in a floor of white plastic tiles (essential for a textile artist because they can be kept perfectly clean) Polly Hope has avoided any 'decorating', letting the building's uplifting scale and her own hangings speak for themselves. A couple of curvy Thirties mirrors, a row of figures on a windowsill and plenty of outsize plants — and the huge place looks lived in.

Bedrooms in the urban cottage style may hover between the primly charming Jane Austenish, and the riot of frills in the Laura Ashley manner, but unlike their country cousins they invariably have fitted carpets, central heating and, more often than not, their own bathrooms. Almost obligatory is a four-poster bed, as elaborately caparisoned as cash permits, lots of old lace, a proper dressing-table with silver topped bottles (mostly empty) and two little lamps with frilly shades.

In the United States, though, where early settlers fought an arduous battle against nature as well as droughts, Red Indians and cattle rustlers, a whole new, vigorous cottage architecture has been created. The styles of many homelands, plus a more expansive, assertive, big-thinking approach natural to colonizers of limitless acres, fuse into buildings more virile than cosy, more rugged than cute. From the earliest Keeping Rooms of Puritan settlers, through the staid farmsteads of Pennsylvania and exuberant rusticity of log cabins in the Adirondacks, right down to the woodbutchers' houses of California in the Sixties, there is a fine native tradition of honest building, using local materials, mother wit and—in many instances—an apparently overflowing bounty of neighbourliness or 'helping out'.

Ingenuity, making out against all the odds, lends a special gutsiness to this strand in American building, and its influence is as discernible in the aristocratically architectural creations of an innovator like Frank Lloyd Wright, whose organic buildings spill outcrops of bedrock over a living-room floor, as in the anonymous, lovingly assembled, *ad hoc* creations of the

woodbutchers of the hippy generation, tailoring their extraordinary nests, like mystic magpies, into the forks of giant trees or across a boulder-strewn stream. There is a freedom, as well as a pragmatism, about these buildings, which taps a new and lively vein in the vernacular tradition and makes the old world cottage, huddled burrow-like round its central hearth, seem cramped and limited in its horizons. Set against the hand-hewn machismo of typical American cottage building, is the formidable femininity, tight-laced but arms akimbo, of the American woman, who was first to champion—in *Ladies Home Journal*—the pioneering architecture of Frank Lloyd Wright on the one hand, and the unarguable benefits, in the first servantless democratic society, of labour-saving technology like central heating. Natural heirs of this double-stranded inheritance are the new generation of pioneers, well-heeled mainly but often genuinely simple-lifers, who find themselves a holiday home out in the sticks somewhere—an old barn, the remains of a ranchhouse, a stable—and fall to work with all the zest and energy of their forebears. Of course, they install central heating and all mod cons, but also they insist on enormous freestone hearths for blazing fires, and care enough about local traditions to redden their floor planks with the local clay, or restore painstakingly, the stencilled ornamentation discovered when paper in an original cupboard is stripped for the first time in maybe a hundred years. The vigour, respect and thoroughness with which some of America's new cottagers approach their inheritance is altogether admirable—a lesson in sensitivity to those older countries who bowdlerize at will much of their modest vernacular architecture.

Another version of the old-barn-into-country-retreat story, with variations. Magnificently picturesque as the great beamed roof looks to be, the emphasis down below is on a more streamlined, svelte, city folks image— tailored white slip covers, countless vases of beautifully arranged flowers, handy lamps and tables for creature comforts, tall, airy and expensive glazed French doors opening out in all directions to the great American outdoors. Super cottage, not modest cot, but with a spanking freshness that should make for comfortable weekending.

New World Vigour

The American style that gets into the glossy magazines tends to be the style imposed on their wealthy clients by American decorators and designers, whose crackling professionalism makes their British counterparts look like dilettantes. Even in the world's richest country, it must be exceptional to have to take the Picassos and Braques into account when planning a room scheme. Plan is the operative word—American decorators do not share the European predilection for places that slowly grow together, like the proverbial college lawn that only needs cutting and rolling for five hundred years to get it the way it should be. An American interior decorator will present a client with a handsome portfolio, colour schemes, fabric swatches, furniture plans, 'accessorizing' all figured out down to the light switches and door handles. Such professionalism is admirable and it invariably delivers the goods on time, well up to standard. Inevitably, too, except in the most skilled hands, it makes for a certain sameness, a Transatlantic Style which is not always the same as style.

American interiors are much more adventurous than British ones. When they go for something, whether it's freaky ornamentalist exercises in spoof classicism, restoring old houses in elegant Southern cities, or outfitting spacious new buildings, they go the whole way. American interiors sometimes lack subtlety, but they have real impact. Colours, for instance, are used with bold freedom: not dirty, muted, European shades but bright, brave, strong and lots of them. Grass green carpet vying with the lawn outside, floral prints of seed-packet intensity for curtains and slip covers, with maybe a chair or two in a plain shade—but a bright one—chosen from the print. Shabbiness has no poetic charm, except here and there in the pockets of old colonial lifestyle. When some legendary lady like Gloria Vanderbilt or Lee Radziwill goes overboard for canvas covers or gingham, she won't try it out on one or two pieces, it goes over everything in sight. This makes for a sort of just-unwrapped freshness and crispness, as cheering to the eye as a fruit salad. It also helps to explain why so many American interiors do not have the air of evolving, they seem to have arrived in one astonishing package, complete down to the matching sets of towels, and the elaborately co-ordinating pillowcases, sheets, duvet covers.

Two quite different facets of the American style seem to me to express great individuality and flair. The first is a breezy, sporty casual effect, as evident in their interiors as in their fashion, which has its sources in phenomena as diverse as Frank Lloyd Wright, cowboy movies and sneakers.

Clear pale bright colours, pretty without being too sweetpea, inviting sofas, bits of Americana prominently displayed, but transcending the detail an overall crisply upbeat effect, light, bright and positive, are all elements I associate with a countrified American style. All is pristine, managing to epitomise the casual and carefree without descending to the slipshod.

Components of American style re-establish themselves in this light bowl of a living room—casual wicker furniture, puffy cushioning, yards and yards of crisp patterned cotton, white-washed bricks, flowers. Easy, colourful, friendly—rooms like these go right along with a style of generous, uncomplicated hospitality.

It has given us open-plan living, low-level seating, the coffee table, dinettes, streamlined kitchens. A few European *cognoscenti* had similar ideas in the Thirties thanks to the Bauhaus and the modernists, but it was America who picked up the elements so suited to its ideal lifestyle—relaxed, outdoorsy, democratic—and popularized and humanized them. Like the barbecue, low-level seating is here to stay and the influence it has had on contemporary furniture design is obvious to anyone who has searched for new bedside tables for an old four-poster bed, or cheap mass-produced occasional tables to go either side of a nineteenth-century sofa built for people who sat upright with their feet together. Furniture of this scale looks oddly dwarfish in high-ceilinged rooms, but the contrast of scale is not displeasing and certainly the effect is casually inviting. With this relaxed furniture, carefree, tough, workmanlike fabrics go best. Hence the boom in recent years in fabrics which once would have been unthinkable in polite drawing-rooms—natural canvas, cotton duck (the favourite fabric of American decorator Billy Baldwin), denim, suede-finished cotton. Informality in the basic furnishings throws an unexpected emphasis on whatever else you put in the room, whether these are priceless paintings or a loving collection of American folk art curiosities. Lighting is a big part of the strategy—pinpoint lights that beam dramatic, modelling light on to statues or the diffuse lights that delicately 'wash' a wall hung with noteworthy shapes, pictures or textiles. The real breakthrough here is a very American ability to see things with a fresh eye, find beauty in unexpected places (think of Warhol's can of beans) to rout us out of our jejune preconceptions.

Another American style which has shaped things around us, is what we call loosely 'early American', meaning by that a homespun, slightly quaint, strongly parochial (as compared with sophisticated metropolitan) look which survives in painted furniture, pottery, stencilled walls, floors, exquisite patchwork and appliqué quilts, naïve paintings and touchingly hand-hewn, carved implements and utensils. Most of this dates back to the late eighteenth and early nineteenth centuries and it expresses the modest but sincere affection for colour and quality of hard-working folks, small farmers, settlers, shopkeepers, with a simple eloquence that speaks directly to people today. Of course, much of what we call 'early American' is derived from European traditions, brought over by English, Dutch, German, Scandinavian and other immigrants. But out of the melting-pot of cultural influences, certain strongly American utterances can be discerned—I am thinking of such things as Shaker furniture, the great Pennsylvanian Dutch barns with their painted 'hex' signs or the bold colours and designs of Amish quilts.

It would have been a typically New World unaffected gutsiness which made these latter things inspiring to the American avant-garde. But there is also a softer, homier aspect of the early American theme which fostered the revival of interest in stencils, painted furniture, floor cloths, and encouraged thousands of women to try their artistic impulses on those most patient of crafts (even when using sewing-machines), appliqué, patchwork and quilting.

America's respect for, and curiosity about, its own past has led to a worldwide rediscovery of the crafts which left the Old World with the earliest settlers and which until now have been sunk in underestimation.

Quaint, formal, gutsy, this wainscotted early American parlour marks both the new country's debt to European and classical tradition—slender classical pilasters, formal eighteenth-century furniture, an oriental rug—and its own lively independence, symbolized in the graining of the panelling and door, which has a naive swagger about it quite new to the patient art of simulating wood in paint. American graining and marbling has a bold freedom of effect which is attributable, one expert tells me, to the much wilder figuring and markings of the native timber and stone. Note too the simple but effective fireplace—bolection moulding framing a sturdy, unpretentious hearth of brick.

Foreign Parts & Formative Pasts

The need to make comes first but the urge to decorate follows hard on its heels. Having discovered how to make jars and platters of sun-dried clay, for storing, carrying and cooking food, primitive people then found that by pressing seedpods, thumbnails, or pointed sticks into the wet clay, they could make pleasing marks, still more attractive when organized into patterns. They may have had additional reasons for pattern making, like identification or a superstitious sense that patterning a storage jar with ripe seedpods would help the corn to ripen next time. However, I am sure anyone who has felt this decorative urge will share my belief that they also made patterns because they enjoyed doing so, and felt proud of the results.

It is a mark of an evolved civilization that it can buy time to be creative. With an army to keep the peace and a slave population to do the work, it is no surprise that the élite of ancient Egypt should have lived in fine buildings, their walls vividly painted with naturalistic scenes, their courtyards cooled by fountains and pools and their furniture of such streamlined elegance that it has inspired designers from classical Greek times to the present day. What the Greeks derived from the Egyptians by way of models and inspiration is nothing, however, to what later ages have derived from classical Greece. Whether or not the classical column with its plinth, shaft and capital alluded to the human body, it established proportions for building and decorating which convince the eye and are appropriate to the human scale. Not only do the parts of a Greek building interrelate harmoniously, they form a space in which people feel the right size, neither dwarfed nor circumscribed. To this day the classical device of dividing walls horizontally into dado, infill and cornice or frieze—corresponding to the three parts of the column—is one which gives a room a look of stability, dignity and completeness. Evidence suggests that Greek interiors were not luxurious, having floors of beaten earth and walls painted rather than sheeted in marble or mosaic, but their furniture—as shown on urns—was finely made and elegantly proportioned, and would have shown to advantage against a dado painted in their favourite colours, rich red, yellow ochre or black. The Romans copied Greek models, and elaborated on them, enriching interior surfaces with precious materials and painted decoration, as was seen when the first complete classical interiors came to light in Pompeii.

Classical models remain the most powerful influences whether one goes back to the originals, to their Renaissance, or to neo-classical interpretations.

The garden room from the House of Livia, wife of the Emperor Augustus. Dating from the first century B.C. this vivid mural painting of an orchard with wilder countryside stretching beyond to a sky of Italian blue, was done in a technique closely resembling fresco where colours are laid into wet lime plaster. This attractive room refers impressionistically to the classical system for wall decoration, with dado, infill and frieze dividing walls in a balanced, proportioned way.

Motley and mingled as a bazaar, the contents of this room could stand for today's eclecticism, historical and geographical, taken to very personal limits. The home of a Brazilian artist based in London, there is a suggestion of South American ferocity about some of the artefacts, not to mention the shaggy fur against blood red walls, which is oddly but interestingly discordant alongside the Chinese porcelain figure. Rooms like these are like private theatres where one cannot always follow the play. Powerful, but puzzling.

Their authority, in terms of a sense of proportion so well founded it appears inevitable, permeates every detail of a traditional room, from its overall proportions to the depth of the pelmets over the curtains, to the size of the mirror over the mantelpiece. Subtracting any element of the system, such as the cornice or fireplace, or introducing furniture made to a different scale, usually creates a feeling of unease.

But, of course, innovators in every area of house design have fought to escape the classical mould and break new ground. The rococo with its playful sinuosities, Art Nouveau with its 'squirming line', the Victorian High Goths with their medievalizing passion, were all attempts to burst the bonds of classical strictness and purity. This century has tried harder than most, with Frank Lloyd Wright pioneering ruggedly individual 'organic' houses which grow out of their setting, Lutyens delving back into vernacular building types and the Modernists designing machines for living to house the citizens of a machine age. Such was the creative vitality of their best work that it did permanently enlarge the vocabulary of architecture and interior design and we can now accept a much wider variety of styles as both beautiful and appropriate to daily life. Such, however, is the irreducible vitality of the classical models that their influence keeps on surging back, if indeed it was ever very far away. This being the age of spoofs and send-ups we have the quote classicism unquote of the ornamentalists or post-modernists, with polystyrene columns supporting nothing and egg cups instead of finials or capitals. Classicism with a snigger rather than a whimper but certainly not with a bang. Interestingly, the most attractive and liveable post-modern habitation may well be the Californian Elemental House designed for himself and family by Charles Jencks, architectural historian, critic, polemicist and the man who coined the phrase 'Post Modern'. Full of classical allusions given a topographical twist, like telegraph poles standing in for doric columns, the jokiness is of an erudite academic sort. The house, split up into four pavilions representing the four elements, is also fastidiously elegant within and without, with a delicate prettiness of colour which in no way detracts from its elaborate iconography.

Interior design is in a state of constant flux but in this confused world, one can still impose a certain order by a process of intelligent selection. One can mix French antiques with Bauhaus classics in a nineteenth-century mansion flat, or paint Palladian inspired murals on the walls of a Victorian basement, or cram museum pieces into a one-time labourer's cottage, or sleep on a futon and drink from stacking plastic mugs in a medieval gatehouse. How effective and coherent this eclecticism appears is the measure of the individual's nerve, enterprise and imagination. In a word, their style.

An eclectic culture, which ours is, is not only open to the influence of historical styles (style in depth) but geographical or ethnic styles (style across the board). The influence is not so uncritical as it was during the hippy diaspora of the Sixties, when every wall bore trophies from Katmandu, Bali and Fez; and remote country districts were peopled with new primitives, building themselves wigwams, mudhuts or stone crofts along approved ethnic lines. Aboriginal style is hard to keep up in cold countries. But the hippy movement helped, I think, to make us less insular, opening our eyes to some of the artistic riches available in the global market-place. We have learnt more since then, becoming more critical and more appreciative in the sense of properly understanding. Exhibitions together with many specialist stores importing ethnic or exotic goods, give everyone the opportunity to tune in to the subtleties of such diverse things as ikat weaves, hand-knotted Eastern rugs, Chinese embroideries, Japanese origami or porcelain, African basketwork and carvings. Casual browsing does not make experts or scholars, but rather as sampling a variety of vintages at a wine-tasting educates the palate, so seeing and comparing the products of different cultures limbers up the aesthetic faculties.

'Rome . . . was tasteful, not profuse.'
ROBERT ADAM

Poignant in its simplicity, this corner of a typical Shaker room is a taking illustration of the New England sect's belief that tidiness is next to godliness. It also shows the degree of aesthetic refinement that gifted people can achieve while aiming at the purely functional. Everything the Shakers made is exquisitely spare in shape and line, yet completely adequate to the needs it serves—the rocker rocks, the small table stands sturdily on its tripod, the tiny round drawer knobs are perfectly judged for pulling, the paddle-shaped mirror attachment hooks over a standard wall peg. It is not difficult to see why this pared down craftsmanship should have had a lasting influence on contemporary design.

Exotic influences are nothing new, of course. They have been creating ripples in the cultural pool since at least as long ago as the Crusades. Chinese lacquer and porcelain, arriving via the Far Eastern spice routes, led to an outbreak of chinoiserie in the seventeenth and eighteenth centuries. Charming little boudoirs, where ladies sipped the exotic new drink, tea, from handleless cups, were hung with imported hand-painted Chinese silk or paper. Young ladies took up 'japanning' as a hobby, painting willow-hung bridges and coolie-hatted figures in sampans copied from pattern books on to firescreens, writing boxes, tables, in imitation of oriental lacquer. It would be hard to find a more attractive example of 'Chinee' inspired decoration than the wide vestibule, hung with pink paper painted with blue bamboo fronds and embellished with a frieze of crinkle-crankle fretwork strung with tiny gilded bells, that runs the width of the Prince Regent's Brighton Pavilion. If chinoiserie was frivolous, Japaneserie, arriving towards the middle of Victoria's long reign, was adopted with a Victorian earnestness. The story of Hokusai prints arriving in this country fortuitously, as wrapping paper for porcelain, has a smack of dealers' blarney about it, like the recent legend of flatweave Bessarabian rugs—currently sought after—originally making their way into the West as coverings stitched round valuable knotted-pile rugs.

The rarefied simplicity of Japanese style, which made such an impression on the High Aesthetic movement, undoubtedly influenced architects like Charles Rennie Mackintosh, whose Glasgow School of Art is one of today's most admired buildings. It inspired, too, designers like Mackmurdo and Voysey, who produced furniture of spare elegance and fabrics whose formalized plant and flower shapes recall nothing so much as printed or embroidered kimono silks. Twentieth-century influences stem largely from Europe, with 'de stijl' and Bauhaus ideas affecting every area of design well into the Fifties. At this point, however, they merged with what is now

Impossible to imagine an interior prettier, more sparklingly frivolous, more apt to raise the spirits of all beholders than the Brighton Pavilion's magical Long Gallery, with its painted glass skylights, tasselled lanterns, and playful variations on the bamboo theme — painted bamboo, in celestial blue on vivid pink, for the wall hangings, gilded bamboo for furniture, cast iron bamboo for the staircases. Incredibly, Victorian improvers painted over this delicious fantasy in orange and pea green.

called 'Scandowegian', all blond wood, simple lines and nubbly handweaves, which became standard uniform for open-plan living spaces as well as new building in the public sector, from office reception areas to psychiatric centres. The provincial insipidity of Scandowegian was soon challenged by a new school of Italian design, which seemed able to infuse racy, streamlined sex appeal into anything from typewriters to sports cars.

Italian design, however innovative and luxurious, tends to be expensive and élitist, too. As geographical or imported influences go, it never made the impact on current lifestyles that the ethnic look did, during the Sixties and Seventies, thanks largely to young flower children backpacking round lesser known parts of the world in search of cheap hash, enlightenment, and first-hand experience of global village life. What might be called the kasbah look, combining Indian and Middle Eastern elements in romantic confusion —rugs, heaps of cushions, embroideries, pierced and carved wood, brass, mirrors, scented candles, joss sticks—has been a strong influence on interiors over the past twenty years, as well as encouraging a revival of the 'pattern on pattern' approach, where layer after layer of pattern and colour are heaped upon each other to create a sensuous richness reminiscent of the Garden of Allah described in the Koran. Not so different either, in its hothouse exoticism, from the *fin de siècle* atmosphere, all drapes and drama, generated by figures like Sarah Bernhardt.

But the natural, effective route to a keen, discriminating sense of local or national styles, remains what it has always been—travel. It is not till one is bodily there, receiving sense impressions on all sides, that one begins to find one's way around a foreign culture, learning to distinguish between the true and the tawdry and homing in on the essential and the best. Everyone should be encouraged to fall in love with some foreign part at least once, preferably while still young enough to be impressionable to exotic inspiration.

Whoever commented that Mackintosh's interiors could only have been inhabited by 'slim gilt souls' had a point. The extraordinary delicacy and refinement of his pale rooms, with their fragile, flower-like decorative shapes are easier to imagine transplanted to Kyoto than in their home ground, gritty Glasgow. The Mackintosh style is instantly recognizable as in the gently weird colour mixtures like mauve and pea green, the beautifully thought out detail in such things as lighting, shelving, glazing, door furniture. If his interiors reveal a Puritan aesthete, the exteriors are in a tougher idiom altogether, and it is the inventive power and coherence displayed there that have made him a cult figure on a par with Soane for today's architects and designers.

Camp, Retro or Kitsch

One thing these three, frequently overlapping, aspects of contemporary style have in common is a strong element of self-parody. Sending oneself up is a joke best played straight, or at least straight faced, because that way the onlooker is never quite sure whether he has got the joke or it has got him.

Two of the first, and now internationally known, performance artists, Gilbert and George, dress in a subtle parody of a Fifties bank clerk—short back and sides, quiet suits with loose but not baggy trousers, neat shirts, plain ties. Their house is painted brown and cream, an early Georgian building as dowdy and neat as themselves. One could easily take them, as they hurry along in step, for a couple of what the hip generation called squares. In the East End of London where they live, where Cockney and Bengali rub shoulders in a curiously frictionless alliance, they probably are seen as squares, if they are seen at all, because in that world of gaudy colours and self-advertising flash, they have made themselves invisible. An unobservant outsider would sense perhaps that their correct duality was a little strange and write them off as harmless eccentrics, wearing their fathers' suits. Anyone into style, however, whether or not they recognized them, would pick up at once on the joke, which is that they are squares squared, too demure, synchronized, self-effacing to be anything but an act. Yet the act is real, is how they live, walk about, eat side by side in a market porters' café, scarcely speaking but alert and communicating. The Gilbert and George phenomenon, which is very much of our times, illustrates or personifies much of the ambiguity which collects around the Eighties version of the dandy.

To be a dandy, defined by the *Oxford English Dictionary* as 'a fop, an exquisite', is not quite what it was when Beau Brummel, wit, arbiter of elegance in an elegant age, personified the word. Brummel was the archetypal trendsetter. He made Bath the fashionable resort, exerted immense influence over the mercurial Prince Regent, scrubbed himself from top to toe every day, and launched a style of impeccably understated masculine tailoring, of sober colour and flawless cut and finish, which has epitomized gentlemanly garb to this day. In contrast to the peacock finery of previous male attire, the Beau prompted a new ideal, of extreme fastidiousness, clothes that depended on cut and fine but unshowy fabric rather than bright colour and ornamentation for effect. On the other hand between the Regency Beau and the deliberately dowdy Gilbert and George there are points of resemblance. Sartorial under-

There is so much of the swashbuckling dandy about George Melly himself, with his hats, cigars, fancy shirts and expansive grin, that the subdued monochrome of his London sitting-room comes as a surprise. Creamy yellow paint blanking out everything (even the marble fireplace), taupe-coloured chairs, pale grey carpet. It establishes the right retro mood for his collection of Thirties lamps, tables, figurines. It doesn't fight with his prized paintings. And it sets him off a treat. Paint suggestion: Dulux Matchmaker Appledore vinyl matt and gloss.

The young owners of this egregious example of kitsch live in it as chirpily as robins in a da-glo nest, in case you were wondering. They put as much time and effort into cheerfully outraging every canon of boring good taste as other people do into keeping up with the Joneses — seeking out violently patterned carpeting, running up cutesy gingham curtains, pasting up leopard spot paper and painting the marble fireplace bronze. Part of the joke is that the basic room is a prim period (early nineteenth-century) piece, complete with cornice. With so many other double takes around, that one barely raises a knowing smile.

statement for one — they have simply taken theirs a few stages further. When well-dressed men wear understated, Brummel-influenced, Savile Row suits, the only way to be even more understated is to dress down, or Retro.

To a dandy, style is not an excrescence, a 'look' one tries on for effect, but something closer to a philosophy of life, a means of shaping that exasperatingly fluid and chaotic substance. When Oscar Wilde pronounced that he abhorred nature for being so middle class he was voicing a real dandy fear as well as being wittily Oscar. Dandyism, of the sort expressed by retro, camp and kitsch style, needs a fly urban audience quick to pick up allusions and ambiguities or the joke misfires.

Visually, where room decor is concerned, all three styles have an element of the theatrical, of exaggeration. One high camp dining-room I remember has walls and ceiling covered with tortoiseshell patterned vinyl, shiny as patent, and sideboards massed with a typically high camp 'arrangement' of carved ostrich egg shells, buffalo horns in silver mounts and assorted small animal skulls. These jokey emblems have replaced grinning blackamoors on pedestals as the chic leitmotiv of high camp decor. Fantasy paint finishes are ideal for this style, being at once theatrical and illusionist and mercifully un-middle class if taken right over the top, with at least three varieties of *faux marbre* (*faux* is a popular word in these circles), rows of matching obelisks, and a *trompe-l'oeil* ceiling. These are after-dark places, excellent venues for parties. Camp, shading off into kitsch, is a favourite role of pop stars, who are heavily into ambiguity at every level. Adam Ant's flat is a prime example of fantasy finishes, everything including most of the furniture, stippled or ragged or marbled in — dandyish touch — the palest, quietest greys and blues.

The surreal, either in decor (lop-sided fireplaces, painted on) or in unexpected placing of familiar fixtures, slots in under camp or kitsch depending on the emphasis. Architect Piers Gough makes a feature of a pedestal basin standing (shades of Marcel Duchamp's notorious loo) like a lost thing in the middle of his bedroom. Designer Tom Brent's house in dockland, designed by himself, features a wonderfully kitsch curving staircase fanning out into his living-room, which seems to be pleading for Mae West.

Kitsch tends to be the bad taste of one generation, rediscovered with hoots of glee by the next. It applies more often to things than decor, perhaps because an entirely kitsch decor implies flights of fantasy difficult to sustain or indeed to live with; also to be kitsch, a room should be a bit sleazy, which might get depressing. Ten years ago a Thirties tiled fireplace, jettisoned on sight by every right-thinking person, would have been kitsch, especially if dressed up with a butterfly-shaped mirror and a crinolined doll designed to sit over the telephone. All these, naturally, are becoming collectors' items.

Retro may have elements of camp and kitsch but is more self-consciously backward-looking in style terms. Not too far backwards, though, otherwise it just becomes straight antique. The joke, or ambiguity, of retro is that it concentrates on a period which the general public has not yet rediscovered, which means any time from the Thirties onwards. If the period reconstruction is flawless, the joke arises that many a visitor, unversed in these nuances, will take it all for real and embarrassingly old fashioned and not know how to react. Besides this recondite pleasure, there is the solid satisfaction of knowing that one's retro decor, bought for a song in flea markets, is appreciating in value every minute.

The Fifties live on, enshrined in the lovingly assembled furnishings of this retro gem which gives a new dimension to the notion of 'period' style. Laugh if you like — the last laugh will be with the tireless compilers of this slice of instant history, pictured in clothes to match. The way we are re-cycling our past, the Fifties must be poised on the brink of re-discovery, and all those whimsical pottery beasties will be snatched off junk stalls by all the people who didn't believe it could happen till it did.

'Eclecticism is our taste; we take what we find, this for its beauty, that for its convenience, and that for its antiquity, and another thing even for its ugliness: thus we live among flotsam, as if the end of the world were near.'

ALFRED DE MUSSET

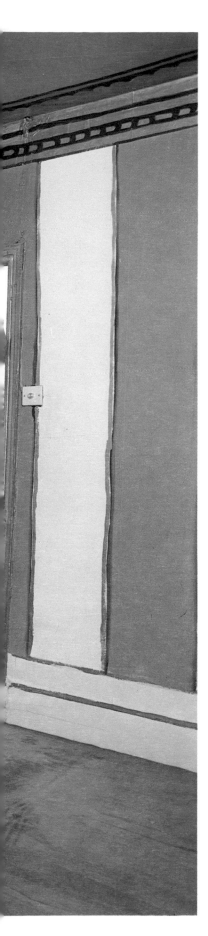

Student Style

To be poor and young has never been a bar to looking stylish. If anything the reverse is true, especially these days when the pursuit of style is one way the individual cocks a snook at the computer age. What the young lack in cash they make up for with energy, resourcefulness and flair, plus a sensitivity to the *Zeitgeist* which has something to do with being out and about in a subculture where news travels fast.

What seems to have stood in the way of students and their peers doing great things in the decor line before was the fact that they were living in college residences or overfurnished digs or bedsits where a free hand with the paint brush is frowned upon. But this situation is changing. Instead of moving into college digs, more and more students are clubbing together to pay the mortgage on a house. Instead of making for bed-sit land, more and more recently ex-students are putting themselves down for, and getting, council flats—usually the ones other tenants object to because they are too many floors up or dark or old fashioned with funny shaped rooms. But who ever let a few pitiful objections like that cloud their excitement and pride in achieving that cornerstone of independence—one's own roof over one's head? The savvy of this rising generation shows as they arrive at dawn in this season's cheapest street market, scour local papers for ongoing jumble sales, investigate the contents of every skip, the attics and basements of abandoned, boarded-up houses and make a special detour the night before the rubbish truck calls on the chance of landing a discarded gem. They are into all the sources of cheap furnishings, like fruit and veg markets for wooden pallets (base for futon), plastic crates (neat storage unit) or office furniture emporiums in downtown areas for metal filing cabinets, desks, stools and standard lamps buried under brown Windsor varnish.

Nit-picking elders might cavil that there is a certain sameness about the visible results of so much enterprise, perseverance and breathtakingly hard work. But designers and such, who need to find which way the wind of change is blowing, are not so superior. If the advanced style in young interiors—art students or recent ex-students are generally considered the leaders in this field—leans towards walls painted battleship grey, with touches of bright pastels or primaries, floorboards scraped bare and stained mahogany, masses of metal filing cabinets, and bright red plastic venetian blinds, this will be pounced upon as an indicative straw. The fact that they go for Fifties-style free-standing units, little and low, like dolls' house furniture made from matchboxes, on which to proudly stand their junky treasures, such as bakelite

---

This essentially period room enters a whole new ball game via jumbo stripes, purple gloss paint and tasty gilt. I like the idea of painting the ceiling to match the carpet. In its off-beat way, this parodic neo-classical interior makes discoveries from which more cautious people may benefit. Have you ever wondered how your Georgian room would look with a coloured lid of a ceiling?

radios with ridgy, rounded corners, or families of kitsch clocks, is also noted. And so is the—to our eyes—inexplicable charm which these infants of the Swinging Sixties find in the stylistically uptight products of the Fifties. More than one canny student with a few pence to spend has acquired stylistic clout by the simple, logical stratagem of buying what no one else is yet interested in or simply rescuing it when they find it abandoned in the street. If you put together enough of a particular style—good, bad and indifferent—the cumulative effect packs a real wallop. The fact that these styles have probably more to do with expediency than aesthetics, in the sense that cheapness rather than beauty is the criterion, is neither here nor there. What is impressive is the fresh eye discerning potential, and putting together interiors which work, from bits and pieces which an older, indifferent society just junks.

This has, of course, always been a function of the young and skint, to rediscover and revalue what preceding generations have grown blind to. They are only a step behind the artists who find meaning and possibilities in the plastic flotsam washed up on the shores of oceans and banks of rivers, and cryptic icons in a can of beans. What is new, it seems to me, is the speeding up of the process. Once it was assumed that you had to skip a couple of generations before demoded chic could re-establish itself as camp, quaint, or kitsch to begin with and then, with sudden accelerating perception and desire, as authentic, original and perfect of its time and place. Now the time lapse is infinitesimal. Young people seem to get the point of artefacts their parents received as wedding presents a year or two before they were born. They may, this being the age of the spoof among other things, just be pretending or

simply making a virtue of necessity, but early enthusiasms die hard. Ageing hippies still feel buttressed by hair, beads, baskets, ethnic embroideries and hand-made candles. Will today's young avant-garde all be living in grey rooms with red blinds in twenty years' time, and—more rum still—will their children be already trying to make off with their beloved bakelite radios and Woody Woodpecker collection?

The young take chances, blithely, in the pursuit of novelty and an arresting image. They may paint rooms all black, a good foil for mock leopard skin, gaudy laminates, flea-market clothing draped around on screens—a kimono or two, a feathered hat, a few spangled Indian scarves, piles of beads give a raffish actressy air. An American girl studying hat design in London paints all the woodwork in her tiny flat the brightest shocking pink, sprinkles the walls with favourite pin-ups in proper if junky frames and fills in the bare spaces with her own hats perched on a variety of dummies and stands. Things for use, like odd cups, plates, jugs of seed-packet brightness, picked up in thrift shops, are conscripted for decoration too, making a razzle-dazzle patch of colour on their pink shelves against a white wall. Another ex-art student has tasty midnight blue walls and ceiling, silver woodwork (aluminium finish radiator paint) and a silver photographer's umbrella shading the overhead light plus collecting stray drips from a leaky roof—this is a squat. A girl who enjoys pattern and colour grabs up every Indian print bedcover (going cheap in jumble sales and street markets) and staples them over the walls and ceiling and drapes them over chairs, table and bed. The effect is gorgeous, a cut-price version of Tippoo Sahib's fabulous embroidered war tent.

Subtly more grown up, but still exhibiting a penchant for sculptures of buildings, the colour grey, and a monkish avoidance of clutter, this is another version of a prevalent contemporary solution to an accommodation shortage—the gallery sleeping space suspended at one end of a tall big room. It is no surprise that this is the work of architects, The Wilson Partnership.

None of this is intended too seriously, or meant to last, it's the effervescent expression of a passing enthusiasm, natural at the age where everyone is trying on styles like hats to see which feels right. 'Maximum effect for minimum effort' is the motto, new paint goes slap on top of what's there, cobwebs and all. None of that lengthy perfectionism of scraping and sanding and undercoating that inspires their elders to prodigious efforts and immaculate results. But then how many elders would dare paint a room all black, or striped, or give it a silver ceiling? A strong stomach may be needed to actually *live* with some of the results, but outrageous experiment is a seedbed for new ideas, and the gradual discovery that what seemed a fabulous idea is a lurid mistake is a step to enlightenment which the people who never stray from safe pastels, co-ordinated fabrics and careful colour matching, will never take.

The worst, and almost first, room I ever decorated, taught me the most. To cheer this north-facing attic I gave it two coats of an orange emulsion so fiery it made you squint. Ignorant then of the quick tricks like glazes or varnishes which would have made it rich and mellow, as I obstinately insisted on seeing it in my mind's eye, it was months before I clearly saw that it was horrible, an attic inferno. I never got around to putting it right, but the pang of failure set me considering colour, light, texture and appropriateness properly for the first time. It was not till I finally got it right in another room in another house, that my flaring orange mistake stopped nagging me. What colour sense I have began there and I wouldn't mind betting that, in ten years' time, some of the most suavely stunning or delectably pretty rooms I see will be the further flowering of a curiosity and cheek that first appeared wearing brightly striped walls and a silver ceiling.

Two things make cheap or student style appealing, its sheer courage and its humour or fantasy. By courage, I don't just mean the audacity needed to experiment with wild colours but the jaunty optimism that refuses to be got down by little things like leaky roofs, a depressing view and next to no cash. That in itself is stylish and so is the humour which makes a joke, rather than a virtue, of necessity. It is a healthy reminder in a world obsessed by surfaces and superficialities that style starts deeper down, with an affirmative tilt towards life.

PART TWO

THE VENUE

Home, Sweet Home

Home is such an emotionally loaded word that you only have to say or, better still, sing it to feel a slight tug at the heartstrings. To be temporarily homeless is to feel frighteningly vulnerable—a recent survey of stress factors puts it only a little way behind bereavement or divorce as a cause of anguish and profound insecurity. A home can be anything from a shack to a castle, urban *pied-à-terre* to cottage wreathed with honeysuckle. Just to know it is there, your own spot on the globe, is to feel rooted, stronger, independent. Home is where you are most yourself, free of constraint, your own and nobody else's person. The French phrase '*chez soi*', meaning at home but literally 'at home with oneself' encapsulates the true meaning.

We used to be much more anxious about the status of our homes, their location—nobs' hill or downtown—their conformity to local or inherited notions of poshness. Your home placed you socially as precisely as a caste mark. This attitude still lingers on here and there but, broadly speaking, it carries much less force in the wake of the great middle class and professional exodus into new districts in search of cheaper housing, easier mortgages and larger gardens. Radicals may sneer or scold but, in my experience, a dose of gentrification does nothing but good to run-down areas. Dilapidated buildings are saved, dowdy ones spruced up, trees are planted, window-boxes burgeon on all sides, front doors beam under new paint and brass door furniture. Visually, this devoted nest-building wakes up a drab street.

But the new spirit of enterprise does not stop there. The real pioneers are always seeking new spaces to colonize and, encouraged by modern architecture's rethinking of interior space and organization, many people look for unorthodox buildings like factories, workshops, warehouses, schools and shops, to convert into homes and workplaces. Exciting as these wide open spaces feel and look, most of us would probably still opt for something more conventional, preferring intimacy and cosiness to drama, plus the privacy of enclosing walls and doors. Grander, taller terraced houses, Georgian and Early Victorian, are generally recognized as the most elegant, but their size makes them impractical—all those stairs—in these servantless times, and many of them are being converted to make flats or maisonettes. All terraced houses tend to be narrow for their height, and the fact that windows are at front and back only can make them dark and tunnel-like, front halls especially. Terraced houses with back extensions have a more rambling, cottagey feel, which can be very appealing—this is the ideal house for many, though the spaces between the back extensions tend to be dark and dank. Conversions of terraced houses into flats, or the basement flat plus a three-floor house on top, produce varied results, wonderful or appalling depending on whether the conversion was done sensitively or not.

Whatever sort of accommodation you have landed up in, it's a safe bet that it has many things wrong with it, some which you knew about from the start, some which have made themselves felt since you began living there. Ideal homes, in the sense of looking right, functioning perfectly and meeting all your needs, are magazine fiction.

I think dissatisfaction with one's surroundings is useful, and perhaps even desirable, because it starts you thinking of improvements. Letting one's mind play about with alternative solutions is quietly stimulating, creative and can lead to all sorts of brainwaves and nifty problem solving. Improving one's home is exciting and gratifying. I don't think it makes too much difference whether we are talking about putting a cupboard into an alcove or throwing up a glazed extension in the back yard. Either way, the planning of it is absorbing, the doing of it enjoyably alarming and the claiming of it finally for clothes or tender plants wildly rewarding. Ingenious problem solving is, of course, an important feature of style.

Restoration v. Alteration

A few years ago the only inhibitions most people recognized when it came to 'doing up' a place were cash ones or inconvenient building regulations. Knocking through party walls and ripping out fireplaces became something of a national sport. Since then a reaction has set in. Not only has open-plan living run into snags and 'real' fires become an estate agents' ploy, we seem to have rediscovered our architectural past, and realized that a lot of it is worth hanging on to.

Our architectural past has expanded considerably too, so that houses do not have to be listed buildings to arouse protective interest. Anyone interested in style now appreciates that much Victorian and Edwardian building is solid, gutsy and handsome and, instead of suppressing its more idiosyncratic features with the aim of making interiors look 'contemporary', proud owners can now be found sandblasting their cast-iron fireplaces, lovingly stripping tiled surrounds, repairing stained-glass doors and windows, taking carpet up off encaustic tiled floors and parquet and cleaning up old plasterwork. The enthusiasm for art deco and jazz age styles in furniture, ornaments, lighting

The Before (above) *and After* (opposite page) *of my own sitting-room. Original pinky wall colour rubbed on (see p. 163) over a Dulux Siesta vinyl silk base. Problem: how to make the room look tied together, compensate for missing cornice and 'lose' junkyard fireplace. Solution: paint; stencilled frieze; blue painted lines to tighten the room structure; painted marbling for the fireplace.*

and so on has led to a revival of the sort of interior where these period items look their best. So far it's the avant-garde, the serious collectors, who are re-constructing rooms, whole houses, in these styles, but the idea will inevitably catch on. As the rooms get photographed, seen and talked about, everyone else will discover how good they can look. From there it's only a step to rediscovering the Forties, Fifties.

This sort of academic thinking in periods can be pushed too far—period rooms where every last detail is historically correct are liable to look and feel like museum sets. On the other hand, there is a lesson to be learned from the great interest currently being shown in restoration and conservation of old houses. Period rooms, which roughly means rooms in houses built at any time before the last war, reflect their times in all sorts of obvious and less obvious ways—the height and disposition of rooms suiting the scale and shape of the furniture then fashionable, which in its turn often related to the sort of clothes people wore, and so on. Things which look bizarre or hideous out of context—tiled Odeon-style fireplaces in Georgian houses, for instance—look not just right, but best, in their proper setting. The same fireplace, for instance, in a Thirties front room—with a hooked rug in an abstract design in front of it, on top a few silver-framed photographs and a clock, and one of those incised mirrors above—looks appropriate, stylish and good. Throw in a couple of curvy armchairs in uncut moquette and a cocktail cabinet and you suddenly begin to see how the Thirties look hangs together and works. Look through old photos of the period or children's book illustrations (a mine of information to style analysts), and you realize that the exasperating gap above the picture rail (you have been thinking of ripping out the picture rail) which causes so many headaches when papering or decorating was intended to be filled in, decoratively, with a stencilled or printed paper frieze. The same approach is equally instructive applied to houses of other periods—the Thirties are an ideal illustration because so many people live in terraced or semi-detached houses of that time, and because suitable furnishings and accessories are still easy to find and not too expensive.

The point is, the more you find out about the period in which your home was built, the more you know about the way it was intended to be furnished and the more it all makes sense. Once you understand how it was meant to look, you have the choice of deciding to play up to that period style (all the way, or only a little—that's up to you) or to change it. Changes made with understanding are likely to look better. For instance, instead of knocking straight through between the ground-floor rooms of a Thirties or semi-terraced house, which leaves odd unexplained spaces and projections, I would be much more inclined to create a real Thirties-style arched opening between them, even flirting with the idea of decorative glass panels each side. That way you still get more light and increased space and the period character is not impaired. Rather than stripping off the picture rail and decorating the wall space as one surface, which subtly unbalances these rooms, I would certainly experiment with stencilled friezes. Thirties friezes were often of autumn leaves in autumn colours. Dulux are producing some very good imitations of these. Why not concoct your own design, based on Thirties fabric or china patterns? Look at paintings of the period before working out colours that would match the bits and pieces one might collect.

PUTTING IT BACK

Let's assume that I am preaching to the converted. You have just acquired an old house, which has suffered at the hands of a bodger or two, and are wondering how to set about repairing the damage done by insensitive alterations—cornices hacked through for pipes or light boxes, panelled doors replaced with flush ones, fireplaces gone in the main rooms, banisters sealed

Punching double doors through from front to back rooms in an early Victorian house gives more light, space and something of the L-shaped drawing-room feel, without impairing the period character, especially when, as here, the double doors are made to match the original doors in height and joinery detail.

in with ply, some important windows replaced with plate glass—familiar evidence of a misplaced zeal for modernization. You are also quite likely to be thinking of doing some building work or wiring which is going to mean inflicting further wounds on the fabric of the place and are unsure how this can be done without leaving scars. The building work should come first on the agenda and prevention of mistakes here can save you time, money and anguish later trying to put it back to rights.

Jobbing builders—those little men down the road who bring in a few mates for the carpentry, wiring, plumbing and so on—tend to be scornful of all the elements you prize so much, partly because they prefer new lamps to old, partly because taking care not to cause too much damage slows up their work and gives them a lot more aggravation. They are inclined to play dumb and look pained when you protest at finding a set of old cupboard doors, old skirtings or mouldings smouldering in a fire in the yard and say they never imagined you would want a load of old rubbish like that. Or, which is harder to contest, they insist that it was crawling with worm and eaten away with rot. Plumbing, wiring, knocking walls through, indeed most building work, involves pulling a lot of the structure apart—skirtings have to be removed, floorboards pulled up, holes drilled through ceilings and cornices.

Working patiently and carefully much of this can be done without damage, but it does take longer. Unless you are prepared either to get a building firm which specializes in restoration work—they tend to be skilled tradesmen, and it will cost you more—or stand over them while the jobs are carried out and pay for the extra time involved, you might find it worth your while to get a tough friend or two along and tackle the preparatory work yourself. Tell the builders what you are planning to do, ask which skirtings need to come off, what floorboards and which door architraves. They will think you are crazy, and probably try to convince you that it is cheaper to replace it all with sound new timber. Ignore this. It is often impossible to replace old woodwork from standard timberyard stock. Most houses built before this century use wide, elaborately profiled mouldings, their skirting boards are wider and thicker, their floorboards were often an inch or two wider than today's standard widths. It is possible to get new matching mouldings run off by specialist firms, but this can be expensive. It is also possible to make up necessary plank widths for skirtings, by glueing two boards together, but the joins tend to reappear in time. So it is well worth salvaging everything you can.

You will need some tools. A floor jemmy which you hammer in along the boards at intervals, levering up a little at a time, makes lifting floorboards intact a lot easier. A bull-nosed chisel and a hammer will be needed for prising off skirtings and mouldings. In old houses these were usually nailed into small wood noggins fixed along the studs in partition and outer walls. When you locate these—studs come at regular intervals—it is not difficult to tap the chisel blade down behind and lever off gradually. Don't try to free a length in one go as loosening it all the way along makes it less likely to split or crack. Use a felt marker to number pieces as you remove them. Remove door architraves before skirtings. Use a fine-bladed chisel to loosen them from the wall—because skirtings were often rebated to slide under the architrave which went on last. If cornices are going to be cut or drilled through, it might be better to try and remove these too—if they are handled carelessly they may crack and come away in lumps or even lengths. Replacing or

Conscientious restoration can run into problems, like the milk-based paint Dan and Vickie Cruikshank tried in their early Georgian house— milk or casein was a constituent of some old paints and the texture and colour they arrived at is very sympathetic to the panelled room, but when banged it flakes off, hence the lack of pictures. Note how harmoniously a room and furniture of the same period fit together.

remaking is difficult and, again, expensive. If you have time it isn't a bad idea to take cupboard doors, especially glazed ones, off their hinges and store them out of the way while building is going on. All the Victorian cupboard doors in my kitchen ended life on a bonfire despite endless warnings and reminders from me. Yes, they were crooked, yes, they were layers deep in old paint, but it cost me several hundred pounds to have substitutes made, and these, inferior things of thin tongue and groove, haven't the style or sturdy panel construction of their predecessors. You have been warned!

You have now reached the stage of restoration proper. First, make sure just what is missing — often, in the craze for streamlined flat surfaces, bodgers took the easiest way out. Many apparently flush doors are really the original panelled doors with sheets of hardboard or ply tacked on all over both sides. Weight and thickness should tell you — old doors faced off are heavier than standard flush and half an inch thicker. Likewise, banisters are often cased in with ply, the original sticks or balusters surviving in between. A wide chisel should dispose of the stair facings. Just drive it in near the top and lever away. For doors, first unscrew handles, finger plates and bolts, then slip a fine chisel blade in and tap away experimentally. Go easy, you don't want to gouge great chunks out of the old door itself. If, when the door is clear, you find panels cracked or missing, don't worry — this is not difficult DIY work.

GETTING OLD PAINT OFF

Invariably, if a building is old and neglected, a lot of old paint needs to be removed before redecorating. On woodwork, the quickest, cheapest and least disgusting way to zap through it is with a blowtorch. It is worth buying a large one — mine is standard builder's size, holding 2 kg gas, with a nozzle on a flexible, detachable hose. The attachment is a bit pricey, but the gas lasts much longer and costs less than lots of little hand-sized canisters. The flame is stronger, too, which speeds things up. I use a leaf-shaped shave-hook for cleaning out round mouldings, a triangular one for flat surfaces and an old chisel for getting into deep fissures. With a bit of practice and care one can burn paint off without scorching the wood beneath, though since this is usually going to be repainted (the stripped pine craze is receding) a few black marks won't matter. What does matter is getting back to clean wood — so scrape off the crusty deposits that the first burning leaves behind while it is still soft, and sand well before painting.

Caustic baths are a trouble-free way of getting doors clean *but* the acid loosens the old glue and, in time, the panels will often develop large cracks around the mouldings. I use proprietary strippers for removing varnish, or — the peel-off sort — for cleaning paint off a carved and moulded piece of furniture.

Banisters are the devil to strip, but it pays to take the trouble. Old ones get kicked and chipped new paint will only emphasize their scarred condition. Bare stairs save on carpet money and look good if the wood is in reasonable shape. Very worn treads can be patched, but get a good joiner to do this. Old tacks must be levered out with a tack raiser — a screwdriver tapped in at an angle helps loosen deeply sunk ones. Really vile old paint on stair treads (where it always took a beating) is sometimes best removed by scraping, using a patent paint scraper or a small unbending steel blade. Scrape towards you, with the wood grain. Dark varnish usually yields to scraping, plus a coat of stripper; but if it is really stubborn, paint the treads instead.

STRIPPING WALLS

Recently applied wallpapers respond quite easily to just yanking; or, at worst, to a good soak, and then tugging an hour or so later. Older, more difficult cases may need steaming off, for which you can hire a gadget. If you are

Wall Textures
When repainting old rooms, walls and woodwork, texture is as important as colour in creating a sympathetic effect. Gloss paint is too shiny for houses over a hundred years old, and matt vinyls are too flat and dense. Most restorers compromise by using a mid-sheen paint finish (oil-based traditional egg-shell, or mid-sheen alkyd) for woodwork and either a flat oil-based paint (obtainable from specialist firms like J. Keeps, Theobalds Road, London WC1) for walls. A similar effect can be obtained with a mid-sheen or vinyl silk base on which a tinted glaze can be applied for a decorative finish. The soft effect of distressed finishes is more flattering to old or period rooms.

61

dealing with the original paper, though, you may find that your Victorian paper is varnished, especially if it is in the hallway or dining-room. Your only hope then is to get the varnish off with paint stripper first, then soak and scrape. It is a long, fastidious job and may be easier to simply repaper.

If the plasterwork behind is 'live' (it moves or bulges) it will probably need to be hacked out and patched or replastered entirely. Again, builders dislike just patching holes and usually prefer to hack off a whole wall and remake it with plasterboard covered with a skim coat. Laths and lime plaster were the way old walls were made and very solid they were too, with a slight pleasing waviness of surface that skimmed plasterboards do not match. But this is purist talk and only a searching eye could tell the difference.

ORNAMENTAL PLASTERWORK

Cornices, the carved or moulded plaster band running between walls and ceiling in many old houses, are one of those decorative additions which served a real purpose. Newly built houses tended—then as now—to settle and move a little at first, which meant cracks opening up at the junction between walls and ceilings. Cornices hid this, while strengthening the join and disguising any irregularities, like a slight curve or dip. Almost certainly your cornice, ceiling rose, and any other ornamental work will have accumulated many layers of paint over the years.

Cleaning this off is a real challenge to a keen restorer. It is laborious, patient work, but immensely rewarding when you get back to the original crisp detail. Oil-based, or shiny, paint is best removed with solvent stripper. More often, though, the paint would have been whitewash or limewash, soft, powdery, water-based stuff which must be removed as modern paints will not adhere to it. Soak the whole area you plan to work on, keeping it as wet as possible to soften the old whiting, and then scrape, gouge and dig it out with something sharp like an ice pick backed up by something flat and hard like a worn-down kitchen knife. Old plaster is much harder than you suppose, usually the paint breaks away in chunks leaving a shining white surface, crisp as icing. When cleaned, you may find chips and cracks and these can be filled with Polyfilla. Larger missing chunks can be remade by a handy person with casting plaster. Add water to this in a plastic bucket, stir well, slop it up with a trowel, then smooth and model with whatever you have to hand (a wooden paper-knife or a spatula) but do it fast because this stuff starts hardening in five to ten minutes. If you enjoy this sort of remaking, you could tackle longer lengths — a bit alarming but extremely economical.

Before you embark on repainting plasterwork of this sort, look at a few illustrated rooms of the period. At certain times cornices were painted in contrast colours to walls, with the ceiling a shade lighter. At others, fancy detail was picked out in several colours — Adam started a vogue for this. And at others again the wall colour continued over the cornice. Getting it right for the period of your house could make all the difference in finding the right proportions for your room.

MISSING BITS

If you want to replace fireplaces, make sure they are in keeping with the style of your house. If your house is in a terrace ask neighbours to show you theirs. Any fireplace may look better than a hole in the wall, but correct proportions do help and cast iron, however amusingly art nouveau, is apt to jar in a Georgian room intended to have a simple, chaste surround of marble or stone. Try to find a surround with its grate complete as fitting grates to surrounds is not always easy. Look for fireplaces in demolition yards, skips and architectural salvage firms, leaving actual fireplace shops to the last, as these beauties cost hundreds when they have been repaired, sandblasted and so on. Hearthstones were usually marble, stone or slate, inset into the floor. Tiles came later. Slabs of slate and marble do still turn up, and they are cheaper if bits are chipped off. If larger than the required space they can then be cut and polished up to fit. (Monumental masons do this, quite cheaply.) Failing this, sand and cement can be stained black, trowelled into the space and then polished with a steel float to almost stony hardness and smoothness.

WINDOW FRAMES

Making up windows to match period styles, whether Georgian or mock-Tudor, is a specialist joiner's work and cannot, therefore, be cheap. Once your eye is attuned to details like the slender glazing bars on Georgian windows or the more fanciful late nineteenth-century versions with inserts of stained glass, it is hard to be resigned to a house front stripped of essential decoration. Occasionally you may be lucky, finding old windows of the right type and size in demolition yards or being taken out of a house along the road. Otherwise it's a case of containing your impatience. One comfort is that new windows, sash or casement type, can be inserted easily and quickly, without messing up your decoration.

Doors are easier to replace. Skips are full of panelled doors, but make sure you have the measurements before toting it all the way home. Demolition yards have old doors stacked like books, usually deep in old paint. Size can be adjusted a trifle — shaving off a little or tacking on a bit to bring it up to exactly the right measurements. A good door is usually heavy, made of thick boards. Shutters are harder to find than doors, but worth searching for if they are missing. Leaded fanlights are almost impossible to find nowadays. Specialist firms will make up copies but this will, of course, be costly. Meanwhile you can try cheating, using putty and undercoat or eggshell paint to make up a facsimile on a half circle of plain glass. You might try simply painting, copying the petalled outlines of an original design in your area. It is not totally convincing, but it is fun to do and much prettier than an expressionless and colourless glazed blank.

Patching Up

Don't try to fill large cracks, gaps or holes in old walls with Polyfilla — this wastes time and money and is not sufficiently tough. Sand and cement, bought by the bag, ready mixed, to which Unibond (the builder's friend) is added to improve adhesion, makes a far stronger filler for rough textured walls. On plastered brick use Carlite Browning (undercoat plaster) first, then Carlite Finish for a smooth surface. For filling plastered walls, Carlite Finish plus a little Unibond is much speedier than Polyfilla. Use a small trowel to fill, and rub plaster smooth before it 'goes off' — i.e. hardens. Any final imperfections can be dealt with using Polyfilla but remember to seal filler with an extra dab of paint before repainting walls. Otherwise, the filled areas stand out from the rest.

Problem Rooms

Most rooms, as anyone who has lived in a variety of accommodation knows well, have problems. Some can be solved by clever tricks, some by smothering them, some by a sort of visual balancing act, some by a nifty bit of carpentry. Here are some of the commonest ones with my suggested solutions.

TOO HIGH

Flat conversions in old houses or the insensitive removal of existing features (dados, picture rails or cornices) can leave you with rooms that feel too high for their floor space. You end up feeling as if you were living at the bottom of a cathedral or a well, with furniture and pictures dwarfed by the yawning spaces above. If the room is big as well as tall, this isn't such a problem. Indeed, you should emphasize it and go for a palatial look. It is when it is tall but small in terms of floor space that it feels wrong.

First of all, work out if anything is missing. An eighteenth-century room (on the lower floors at least) would almost certainly have had a dado, or chair rail, running round at approximately windowsill height. A later room, Victorian, Edwardian or Thirties style, might well have had a picture rail at approximately half-way between the top of the door and the ceiling line, though the exact positioning varies with the overall height and the period. Since the areas of wall above and below these horizontal demarcation lines were intended to be treated differently, with different colours, or patterns in one space and plain colours or different patterns below, their removal and replacement by one unified finish easily explains why the room feels too high. If you can afford to restore the missing mouldings, excellent. If you can't, you should recreate them visually, with paint, stencils and colour changes. This immediately balances the room up again. Suppose it's a dado that has gone. Paint either a solid line, rail width, round the room; or stencil a chunky sort of pattern (palmettes, anthemions, or daisies and leaves) round the walls. It is best to continue this elsewhere in the room, round the ceiling perhaps or the doors and window frames, to make it look 'meant'. Paint it in a contrasting colour to the walls. Often this is enough to cut the vertical line. You may need to cut it further by painting the wall below your line a different colour, as it originally would have been.

Painted false panels are another optical trick to cut height and they should be painted in both above and below the dado line. Apart from the measuring there is nothing bothersome about *trompe l'oeil* on this level—a little more white on two sides, a little more umber grey on the other two and the panel

---

Now here is a guy, faced with the problem of blank walls and an aching space above the picture rail, who has set to and created his own artwork. On a yellow-cream, he has stencilled a frieze in terracotta and green, with picture roundels and a splurge of colour behind his chair. Paint suggestion: Dulux Buttermilk vinyl matt for walls; picture rail in Muffin gloss.

Balancing High Rooms
Heavy and elaborate Victorian
cornices were often picked out in
colour or gold leaf (transfer leaf is
obtainable from artists' supply
shops or by mail order from
Stewart Stevenson, 66 Roding
Road, London E5)—instead of
being whited out to match the
ceiling as they usually are today.
Making the cornice more important
can help a tall room especially if
this is balanced by interest at dado
level, such as marbling (see pages
169–170) or false panels (see pages
166–167). A well arranged display
of pictures helps, too, as does tall
furniture—bookcases to the ceiling,
towering overmantels with shelves
as well as mirrors, and high-backed
chairs.

illusion is there. Sometimes the panels themselves are painted a couple of tones darker than the ground colour. It might be buff on cream, grey on off-white, dirty pink on pale pink, grey-green on light green. To dirty colours just stir a little umber into the base colour.

The enormous rooms of the stucco era respond to the same treatments on a larger scale. A wider decorative border painted just below the ceiling or cornice helps to balance them. This frieze technique is the one to use, too, for rooms which would have had a picture rail or which have lost their original cornices, as it both cuts height and creates a little emphasis and interest at ceiling level. The cheapest way to get the effect is to paint the top strip of wall to a depth of between eight and fourteen inches (depending on the overall scale) a different colour from the rest of the walls. Then stencil a suitable pattern all the way round in one or more colours. The blue-green room in my house has a nine-inch wide strip in creamy pink, outlined both sides in dull red and stencilled with an Indian border motif taken from a bedcover, in black, yellow, dull red and blue. In the pinky room, also minus cornice, I am painting a stone-coloured one and stencilling in an architectural sort of motif in grey-green, sepia and off-white to suggest carved decoration. Another way to get the frieze effect if your walls are papered is to paper the top strip in another pattern, similar in colour and tone but on a different scale—smaller or larger—or you can look out for printed borders wide enough to give the same effect.

TOO NARROW

Many front halls are so narrow that they feel like crevasses. They are usually dark too, their sole light coming from a window above the door. If your hall is also very tall, devices like the false panel arrangement work very well, both

Long, lofty and unusually narrow, this room in an ancient Greek island house comes up with several solutions. Paint everything white, magnificent fireplace included, but splash colour everywhere via pictures, cushions, painted chairs. Cut the tunnel feeling further by raising seating area on to a platform (note attractive balustrade) where people can sprawl on generous cushions round a real fire.

cutting the height vertically and suggesting width because of the 3D effect of the two-tone panels. Any trickery which adds an illusion of depth to the walls will help push them out and make the space between them seem wider — trellis, either painted or on wallpaper, gives a feeling of space and so do papers based on the eighteenth-century French *Toile de Jouy* scenic designs. Decorative paint finishes have the same effect — rag-rolling, sponging, colour-washing work particularly well. Paint the ceiling a shade paler than the wall colour, leaving the cornice white. The odd mirror hung on the wall can help, especially if it can be hung opposite a door, so it is reflecting more than the wall opposite. However, unless your look is very modern and you can afford to do it in style, I would avoid mirror tiles or sheets of mirror glass. Mirrored expanses are disturbing somehow, slapped arbitrarily in the middle of a wall. Either the whole wall needs to be mirrored or the glass must be given a surround of some sort to contain and define it. A subtler way of getting the reflective effect would, I think, be to silver the ceiling. Aluminium transfer leaf comes in sheets about the size of a small handkerchief. It is not expensive and is easy to stick on, using gold size as an adhesive. Overlap the sheets a little, to give the pretty tiled look seen on Japanese screens. The foil needs to be varnished to prevent the silvery colour darkening. Varnishing with button polish or orange shellac makes silver leaf look like gold.

The other space-stretching area to think about in narrow halls is the floor. Diagonal lozenges in black and white or another two colours open a narrow space out amazingly. They can be made from vinyl squares, or painted straight on to the boards.

Embossed paper is often found in old houses in front halls, sometimes carrying on up the stairs. Considered objectionable for years, it is now coming back into fashion, being unusually tough as well as decorative in a heavy

Dark walls can look rich, rather than sombre, when you start with a subtle Morris print (as here in the dining-room of that monument to late Victorian 'artisticalness', the Linley Sambourne House in Kensington, London), and then break it all up with groups of framed prints and photographs, a frieze of blue and white porcelain, a flash of gilt and lots of warmly polished wood. It is a strong, handsome look, making much more of the grouped pictures, for instance, than a 'safe' neutral shade.

Victorian style. Stripping off old lincrusta often takes half the plaster away with it. Better, if you find it too dark, to overpaint and then glaze with a darker tone, wiping the glaze lightly off the raised parts of the pattern to give a look reminiscent of tooled leather. Burnt sienna glaze over red would look rich, burnt umber over buff more leathery, raw umber over leaf green distinguished. Above these hang a large-patterned Morris or Voysey wallpaper. A collection of old sepia photographs mounted in plain card and framed in plain oak frames (unfashionable still, so you can often find them in jumble sales or markets) look particularly good hung on these very richly patterned papers.

TOO DARK

Before rushing in with all the lightening, brightening tricks it is as well to consider when and how you will be using a dark room. A basement flat, used mainly in the evenings, could end up looking a bit stark if you make lightness your aim. If the main room faces into a front well and light is short even in high summer, I would concentrate instead on making it vivid and cosy, using warm strong colours on walls, like Pompeian red (light, dullish red), a sunshine yellow or apricot. Basement conversions are so stark as a rule that any texture you can add must help. Use matting on the floor wherever you can, and collect bright rugs, ethnic ones like dhurries and Peruvian hand-weaves, to hang on the walls and drape over the chairs as well as spreading them on the matting.

Mirrors are good, of course, but I usually find hanging them opposite the window, as one is advised to do to reflect light, robs them of all sparkle and

A bathroom could hardly look less clinical, despite bare board floor, rub-a-dub tub and no attempt at comfiness. The riotous wallpaper, its tawny shades picked up in the shiny ceiling paint, has a lot to do with the friendly glow of the place, as do the solidly framed old mirrors and the two pretty swan-necked lights with their light diffusing ground-glass shades.

mystery. I hang them sideways on or sometimes in the middle of a blank space in the window wall, where they have a subtler dissolving effect. Old mirrors, with their glass stained and the mirroring eaten away here and there, have a pewtery tinge I much prefer to dazzling new mirror glass. They sometimes cost much less, too, due to these 'defects'. Why not collect three or four of those deco-style mirrors that once hung above oak or tiled mantelpieces in suburban front rooms? Hopelessly unfashionable a few years ago, these are now collected and hung in a row one above the other, their odd shapes, somewhere between a moth and an old radio set, look pleasing. Mirror tiles used to cover coffee tables also reflect light back dramatically and unobviously.

Basement windows tend to be grim. Large, metal-framed affairs without architraves or sills, their view outward—usually a concreted area—is not uplifting. Ideally, I would fit them with a pierced carved Indian screen to filter the light decoratively and block out the view, but these hardly turn up every day. Bead curtains are another possibility, perhaps with one of those wildly embroidered Indian pelmets above to soften the hard-edged look. More cheaply still, drape several yards of white lawn, sheeting or calico (wash with bleach first to whiten and pre-shrink) over a wooden pole to hide most of the window and make a casual swag along the top.

The darkest room of all, of course, is the one without natural lighting, often a tiny bathroom slotted into the middle of a basement flat. Since it has to be artificially lit, darkness *per se* is not the problem, though claustrophobia might be. Militate against this by using as much indirect lighting as you can, strip lights fixed under wall cupboards, maybe behind a wooden pelmet or baffle run along just below the ceiling. Use mirror tiles round the bath. The French sculptor, César, created a showy, vulgar and wonderful bathroom for himself by setting thousands of fragments of mirror (you could not be superstitious for this) into wet plaster, so the whole room refracts like a vast chandelier when lit up. You could also, aptly, turn a room like this into a grotto, painting it dark sea-weedy colours, with painted weed, fishes (a little gold on their scales) streaming up the walls. Real shells can be encrusted round mirrors but not where you are likely to sit or lean unclothed—they can be painfully sharp. A room with no daylight is unreal to start with, so make this an excuse for fantasy.

Small dark upstairs rooms, usually former boxrooms, need generous treatment to kill that forlorn garret look. A case for floors painted white, with a rug, spriggy paper and co-ordinated curtains and covers, perhaps. Alternatively, paint walls red and stamp a potato-cut border all round in black and white and hang black and white gingham curtains. Gingham checks and pyjama stripes are two classics of the haberdasher era, due for a revival. If it's sophistication you want, though, try a suede-finished wall covering with brushed cotton curtains and covers and use the cheapest aluminium picture moulding to neaten up the edges of walls, around windows and cupboards with prints and photos framed to match. A snug like this also makes a great study. Pillows and chair seats could be covered in fake leopard or zebra. Tarty, but good fun.

Print rooms are enjoying a revival for the first time since their modish appearance in the late eighteenth century. Ladies whiled away the time at their country houses selecting black and white prints, arranging them in attractive groups, and then pasting them down flat on to walls painted in such fashionable colours then as pearly grey, soft light blue, Robert Adam's sunny pea green. Anyone could copy this idea, using any attractive prints, engravings, etchings, mezzotints (use copies preferably, originals might be too valuable), pasted down in formal symmetrical arrangements, with black and white borders (try wallpaper shops, or the National Trust shops) to match. In a small room it looks quaint and charming.

Reflective Surfaces
If you want to play about with reflections but don't want, or can't afford, mirror glass, panels or tiles, you might consider using silver PVC. Sold by the yard, it can be fixed to walls or ceilings with strong wallpaper adhesive. It also helps with sound and heat insulation.

IMPOSSIBLE, AWKWARD, POKY

Impossible rooms, hung with pipes and dissected by fuse boxes, small, lit by miniscule skylights or off-centre windows—the rooms their owners usually describe as gloryholes—*can* be the most amusing to do up if you enjoy a challenge. Trying to make them look like a conventional room is wasted effort—much better to make them look like a lavish little tent. Designer, Diana Phipps, buys bolts and bolts of the cheapest printed cotton (from Indian wholesalers) and staples it on lavishly, smothering ugly features with folds and swags and ruching the ceiling up to a big rosette in the centre (see page 81). Stuck round with the odd picture or mirror and some bits of ethnic tat, the effect is extreme, a touch camp but absurdly luxurious, and altogether a step up for a former gloryhole. You need a good powerful staple gun, but instant changes are supremely appealing and this tool will pay for itself speedily. Use it to fix canopies over beds, curtains that loop back instead of drawing (prettier on many tall, period windows), fabric or felt linings to wardrobes, even upholstery to chair frames. Taking a leaf from Diana's book (literally, her *Affordable Splendour* is full of such transformations) I stapled cheap striped cotton over my bedroom walls and some cupboard fronts in a day and a half. Stretched flat, as it was there, it looks best applied over the lightest weight polyester padding sold by large department stores for padding and quilting. I bought a whole bolt (50p a metre for 100 metres) and, after covering walls and making three pairs of floor-length quilted curtains, I still have more than enough left to drape a four-poster bed, make sets of duvet covers and probably half a dozen shirts.

Another thin, tall room, its shape exemplified by the ducky little Victorian fireplace, gets the brightening and whitening treatment with several coats of just off white (eg Dulux Matchmaker Calico gloss) on the tongue and groove but this is then cleverly opened up by crowds of interesting pictures, primitive, Pre-Raphaelite, or frankly kitsch.

Opposite page: *Some day I'm going to paint lines along the top of the cupboards to match the striped edging shown below the windowseat, and hang a draped pelmet, but meantime I am quite proud of the problem solving shown here. Problem: one window which didn't match up with two shuttered Regency ones, plus no cupboard space. Solution: fitted cupboards, fabric hung to match walls, enclosing a window seat with more storage space below. Quilted curtains in striped shirting soften the effect and tie the whole room up visually.*

Small Space Living

Bedsits are liable to have some of the faceless problems of the boring box. But their crying need is for artful contrivance—to fit all of one's daily activities into one room without too much mess or squalor; and to house all the paraphernalia from cooking utensils to books to clothing in a not very large space which is never generously enough provided with built-in storage. The ideal bedsit would be as neatly and compactly fitted out as an old Pullman sleeper or a showman's caravan. The reality is, however, somewhat different: divan bed, tacky old wardrobe, Baby Belling sitting on a lino-covered table, a sink unit and maybe a couple of Fifties armchairs each side of the gas fire.

It is not worth laying out much cash because you won't be staying long, but the place decidedly needs cheering up and organizing, so that you are spared that strangely sordid juxtaposition of dirty linen and dirty crocks.

INSTANT EFFECTS ON NEXT TO NO CASH

You aren't allowed to, or don't want to, decorate. So buy several of the cheapest printed Indian cotton bedspreads and just drawing-pin these to your walls, covering as much of them as possible. Drape another over the bed, and over the armchair if there is one. These can go with you when you leave and be used for table cloths or curtains at your next stage on. If the curtains are dreadful take them down and put up a pinoleum blind, or bead curtain. An old cabin trunk, painted or stuck with fablon, can serve as a table, stool and hold extra clothes. Push your bed tight into a corner and pile cushions on to it—look for old bed pillows, which can be chopped in two to make one square and one little oblong pillow. Old dresses in markets do nicely for covering them. Lighting always seems inadequate in bedsits. Standard lamps are back in fashion but still turn up cheaply in turned wood or chromed metal. With a strong bulb they can be moved about and give a wide spread of light. Pleat fancy paper to make a shade or try last year's straw hat.

Look for a shop clothing rail of some sort to carry an overspill of clothes—round chromed ones are great. Hat stands are too, but increasingly pricey. If it's getting out of hand, fix a pole in an alcove or across a corner and hang another bedspread in front. If cooking storage space is really inadequate, consider buying one of those Utility-era cabinets (let-down flap, glassed-in doors above, sort of meat safe below). Spruced up, painted maybe, these have a gawky charm and are very useful, taking plates and cups above, cutlery in the middle compartment, pans and tins below. Screw hooks wherever possible, down the window frame, under shelves, on wooden uprights, to suspend

Bright ideas make all the difference when you live and sleep in one small room, like young graphic designer Rozelle Bentheim. Like the box seating she had built round one corner which reveals large storage units when you take off the cushions. Or the venetian blind hung from the ceiling acting as the simplest, but effective, room divider. Paint suggestion: Dulux Barley White vinyl silk.

whisks, sieves and colanders. Haunt jumble sales and flea markets for your buys. As a treat for yourself, if you have any money over, get something new and pretty, like a really nice bed set (duvet cover, sheet, pillowcases) or delicious towels in bright colours. A small amount of self-indulgence is comforting and makes you feel less cramped.

The difference between a small flat and a bedsit is that you are more likely to own or lease it. It may have been fitted out quite comprehensively to begin with but you will probably want to spend some money on it.

Well-designed small spaces can be very civilized but they do need thinking out if activities as different as cooking and sleeping are not to get into a muddle. It's one thing to close the kitchen door on a sink full of pots and pans, not so nice to climb into bed in full view of them. One answer is to make a narrow galley kitchen along one wall, and install folding doors, plain, louvred or pull-down screens, which cover it in completely when it is out of use or in a mess. One small flat I know on the top floor of a Victorian house in North London has the kitchen partitioned off from the living-room space so that it can't even be seen from the bedroom, which is reached through glazed double doors at the far end of the seating area.

One advantage of a small place, apart from being easy to keep clean and tidy, is that one needs so much less in the way of furnishings that one can usually afford to buy the best. Not all at once, perhaps, but gradually. If there is any building or joinery to be done initially, this is where money should be spent first. Good workmanship in the detailing of a small place (decently made cupboards and units, immaculate finishing and making good) pays off immediately in the feeling of ship-shape comfort it gives. 'In a really small

Opposite page: Architect Alan Short's elegant conversion showing the profile of the S-shaped dividing wall and the space-stretching effect of mirrored door beyond—that mirror reflects back another small diamond-shaped mirror stuck flat to the wall in the main room, the sort of gamesmanship ornamentalists delight in.

The plan of Alan Short's top floor conversion shows a triumph of imaginative compression and stylish visual trickery designed to give an impression of lordly space. The style is tongue-in-cheek classicism, pedimented doorway allied to suave painted stripes, an S-shaped partition leading the eye to a door immaculately mirror-tiled, an ingenious porthole window which lets sunlight through into the living-room by day and artfully placed spotlighting (to suggest moonlight) by night. The joinery was professional, but the demolition and decoration is all his own work.

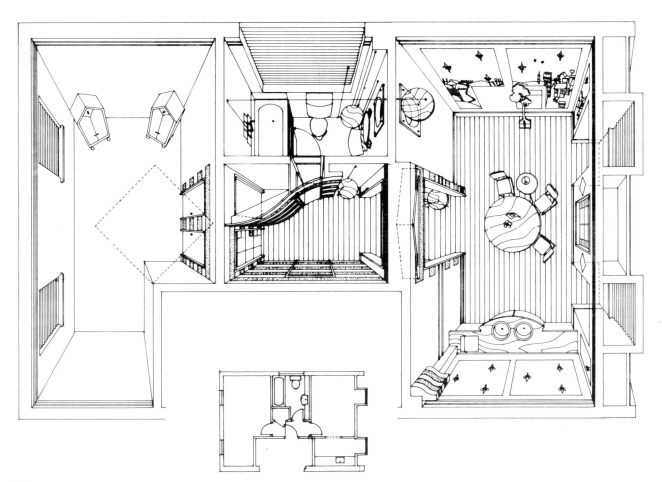

place even the door handles matter—you notice the details more,' one designer told me.

Beds can be a problem, if you don't have a separate bedroom. A single divan bed can be integrated into a room plan quite easily. Pushed back against the wall with built-out bookcase or hi-fi units at each end, it becomes part of the seating. Double beds are intractably large. One solution is to fold them up into a wall unit during the day. Sofa beds, which open out to double bed size, are another, if you are the disciplined sort who leaves time for this every morning. Double futons, which roll up to make squashy low seating, are good if you like sleeping on a fairly hard firm surface (great for the back) and your style is informal. Where there is enough space, a double bed can be set squarely in the middle of the floor, with everything from bookcases to TV to drinks cupboard built round it, to create a sort of lounging island. Problems here are how to get at the bed to make it, and keeping it decently covered when you are not using it. If one is realistic, the easiest solution is nearly always the best. If you can't tuck your bed into an alcove or partition it off behind screens or curtains hung from a ceiling track, have it out in the open. Pushed into a corner, cover it in something tough and good-looking (duvets

Designer Alison MacDonald makes good use of glazed doors in her small, converted Victorian flat to give as much light and illusion of space beyond as possible. Double doors into the bedroom are hung with louvred blinds for privacy—the louvres can be adjusted.

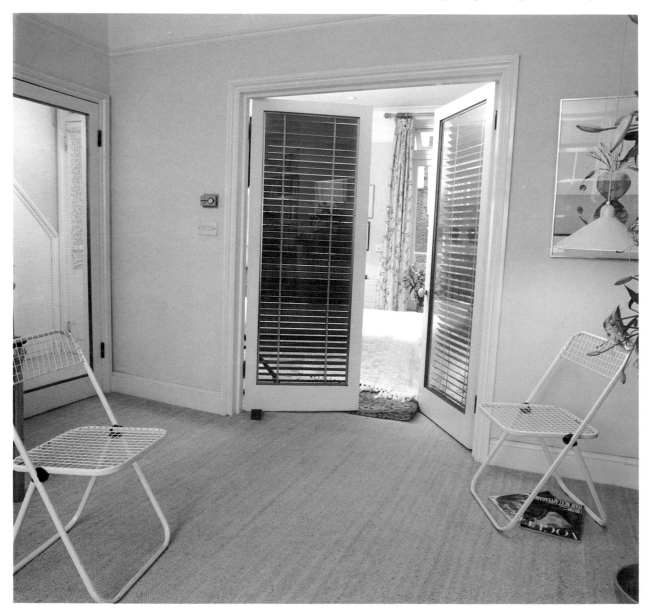

and slipping counterpanes look hopelessly blowzy), add cushions, and maybe a unit on castors along one side. But try and arrange other seating so that the bed is not conspicuous. One new studio flat I saw recently had sofa and armchairs ranged along one wall facing an alcove in which stood, uncompromisingly, a double bed. Perhaps it's my dirty mind but it felt like a blue movie scenario.

The owner's repertoire of visual tricks gives serenity to a crowded living space—pale colours, outsize sofa, light modern furniture and prints, one-colour nubbly carpeting throughout and an overall bright wall colour like Dulux Lily White. Intelligently placed pendant lights dispense with tiny tables and trailing flexes, while shelf units hold all the necessary paraphernalia. Note the obligatory fireplace, in working order.

Alison tucked a tiny, intensely planned kitchen off one side of her living-room, underlining the change of pace with a blind and chic white tiles instead of lace curtains and carpet. A token room divider, waist high, closes the kitchen off visually. Joinery again is immaculate, planning hairsbreadth accurate.

The Basic, Boring Box

All rooms are boxes more or less, but the basic-box room is just that and no more, unless you count a door and a window or two. Usually the result of a tight-fisted conversion or unimaginative speculative building, the basic box has the blank feel of new places unrelieved by anything of architectural interest—no cornice, nooks, bays or alcoves. Such woodwork as it may have is flimsy, skinny skirting, flat doors, built-in units of ply, standard windows with plastered reveals, no sills. The floor is most likely concrete or possibly vinyl tiled. In a new building the ceiling may be finished with prickly Artex, in an older one it could have polystyrene ceiling tiles covering cracks. The sound insulation is terrible because the thin partition walls let all the noise through.

There you have it, featureless, characterless, new, boring, clone of thousands such rooms up and down the country. Not exactly cheery to come home to, but it is your home and you are free to decorate and do it up any way you want to. The good news is that the basic box, the nothing room, is one of the most interesting and fun to decorate. There are no period features to take into account, no charms to emphasize. You can impose almost any style on it and anything you do will be a great improvement. Since it is probably not a very large room either, it won't cost much or take too long.

So where to start? Not, I would suggest, poring through wallpaper books in the nearest DIY shop. Papering basic boxes in one of those feebly patterned papers with a washable finish which turn up in all the cheaper ranges only makes basic boxes look tackier. Wallpaper cut off along the ceiling line underlines the boxiness and a cheap paper here is a false economy—they need a more imaginative approach than the lick of paint and new paper everywhere.

What they need, first, is quality: honest materials with inviting textures, good colours, a touch of lavishness, finesse in finish and detail. If you can't afford good carpet, don't go for cheap stuff that will look depressing in a year's time, choose a sturdy matting in a pleasant biscuit colour, fit it over underlay and bind the edges with webbing and Copydex to stop it fraying. But the first bit to get right is the walls and ceiling.

Consider, seriously, covering up the lot with fabric. Not a hugely expensive furnishing fabric, but any cheap cotton dress fabric you like the design of. Bought from a wholesaler it works out cheaper than wallpaper. A polyester wadding goes on first, staple-gunned in place to give a luxurious padded look and help keep noise out and heat in. Wall-sized panels of fabric, machined together, are stapled on top and the staples hidden by glued-on ribbon,

A room is a room is a box is a boring box very often in today's house-into-flat conversions. But not here, where cool classical columns and sky-blue walls and ceiling dappled with floating clouds open it all up, dramatically. An outstanding example this of ornamentalist style and guile—note tiny gilt cherubs taking the mick out of the clean functionalism of bedside lights.

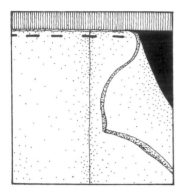

To wrap up a room in fabric first staple a polyester wadding to the walls.

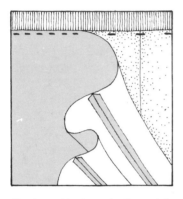

Staple machined panels of material over the wadding and hide the staples with decorative tape.

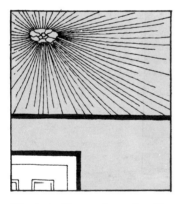

'Tenting' will conceal an ugly ceiling and totally transform a boxy room.

Opposite page: *Tented rooms might have been invented for Diana Phipps, seen here in her dazzling London dining-room with the tools of her trade—yards of inexpensive fabric, staple gun. Diana likes rooms to have punch and chutzpah—and tenting does this dramatically and fast. Here shutters, banquette seating and cushions are covered to match, creating just the glamorously cosy setting anyone would feel flattered to eat in.*

webbing, cotton tape dyed to match, cotton lace, leather strips—choose what suits your fabric. Take the banding down the corners, round doors and windows as well as along the ceiling and skirting for a smart braided uniform effect. If the ceiling has an ugly finish the best thing is to cover it, too, with the same fabric. For smallish squarish rooms, tenting is a possibility, where the fabric is ruched to a central rosette. Otherwise stretch it flat and use a few extra staples to stop it sagging. Fabric-covered rooms look cosy, luxurious and a touch exotic. Having all that real texture around does wonders for a basic box and transforms it into something more precious, like those velvet-lined jewel cases or silk-lined sewing caskets children find irresistible. Considering how grand the effect, it is neither difficult nor slow.

With fabric walls paint any exposed woodwork a flat colour that tones in with the fabric. Doors can, of course, be covered to match the walls, which looks even more classy. Left-over fabric could make curtains (machine quilted for weight and style), table covers, even lampshades (for DIY, see pages 153–155). But resist using it anywhere and everywhere or it may end up looking claustrophobic.

If slick modernity is more your style, nick an idea from designer Eva Jiricna, and try covering your walls with shiny PVC by the yard. It comes in bright colours, should be glued in place with heavy-duty wallpaper paste, and covers cracks, damp patches, everything. Use thin battens, painted silver or a shiny colour, to smarten the edges at ceiling and floor or skirting. Stamped plastic industrial flooring is the obvious choice to go with this, also sold in strong colours and black. If you want the shiny look, but can't afford PVC, take a deep breath and give the walls at least two coats of gloss paint. If you rub the walls down conscientiously, with medium grade sandpaper, before the first coat, between coats, and yet again with finer grade after the second and before a coat of varnish, you will have a fine shiny surface. This is best done with the room empty, swept and the floor sprinkled with water to keep the dust down. Use clear gloss or yacht varnish, bearing in mind that all varnishes yellow or darken in time. They do wonders for colours though. Paint the ceiling matt if it's prickly, shiny if not, and do the woodwork in with the walls to make the room look larger—mean skirtings, architraves and flush doors aren't worth calling attention to anyway.

One more, somewhat traditional, look for the box is the cottagey look. Here, a distressed paint finish supplies the texture for walls. If it's feasible, begin by fixing standard coving all round in lieu of a cornice. Light, easy to cut and fix up and relatively inexpensive, this simple addition will make a great difference visually, softening the boxiness, adding a touch of much-needed class. The joins where walls and ceiling meet are the most unsatisfactory bit of basic boxes—ask any designer. Failing coving, paint a line or stick up a border.

A cottagey effect needs warm, soft colours like apricot, yellow, brick pink or red, depending on the size and outlook of the room. These can be applied flat the usual way, but breaking up the colour one way or another so that the white or off-white base coat 'grins' through is much more flattering to a dull room. Distressing 'lifts' colours and makes the walls look softer, the room appear larger. It is the best trick I know for giving a place instant atmosphere. Sponge the colour on or slap it on loosely with a big brush, so that some brushmarks show. Alternatively, paint it on thick, then stipple off again with a stiff brush for a speckled effect. The simplest finish of all, which I often use, is to coat walls first with a smooth vinyl silk base coat, then using a colour several shades more intense than one wants the finished walls, dab a soft cloth into the paint and gently rub it into the smooth wall surface. This gives a gentle unevenness of tone, which looks time softened and distinguished. (For DIY, see page 163).

A wild, warm orange red glaze, ragged on walls, with print festoon blinds in a similar colour, a collection of brilliantly blue Bristol glass, and lots of nicely framed prints, take all the customary drabness from the tight stairwell space in this small terrace house. Instead of shooting past, one stops to look.

The clever thing with all these blurry, deliberately dappled finishes is to tidy them up around all the edges with a band of contrast colour, an inch or two wide. This can be painted on or cut from coloured paper and stuck down. Or, for a more elaborate effect, stencil a border or buy a printed one. Take the line, like the band in the fabric room, all around doors, windows and up corners to sharpen the room up, give it a little muscle. Another excellent visual trick, suitable for biggish boxes, is to paint false panels. Not *trompe l'oeil*, but the simplest suggestion of panelling (see pages 166–167). Paint the panels a few shades lighter than the surrounding walls and outline each one in a soft but contrasting colour. Nancy Lancaster, a decorating legend, has used this trick in her tiny country dining-room, which is really quite boxy. Off-white panels are outlined in blue on a buff ground, giving a 'finished' effect which compensates for missing cornice and is elegant enough to take a gilded mirror, blue and white china and a miniature chandelier. Flat doors can be panelled to match. Artex ceilings I would find very difficult to live with. One could replaster on top, since the rooms are small enough to make this possible for an amateur. Even if you didn't make a marble smooth surface, it could hardly look worse than what's underneath. Alternatively, cost out the notion of using tongue and groove fixed to battens and painted white to encourage a cottagey look. Instead of the flimsy pinch-pleat curtains beloved of show houses and hung from skinny brass rods I would go for something different

for the windows. Try festoon blinds (best in the bedrooms probably) in spriggy cotton, gingham or cotton lace with pleated blinds or even painted louvred shutters for downstairs rooms.

FURNISHING

With walls and ceiling and woodwork visually pulled together, and given a classy finish and texture, furnishings can afford to relax. Don't spoil things by getting a boring three-piece suite. One large comfortable modern sofa, plus floor cushions, plus a canvas chair or two would be more flexible as well as stylish. Or, if the room suits, try unit seating, wide enough to settle back into, pushed up along a wall or round a corner. Make a low table, large enough to eat at crosslegged, from ply tacked to a timber frame, then covered with tiles—smoky mirror tiles look dashingly different when used in this way. For the bedrooms, try making the bed into a feature. Push it against the wall and hang a draped canopy over it or fake up a four-poster with curtains running on ceiling tracks. Anything which cuts up the boxiness of these rooms is good. Since they lack built-in features like fireplaces or alcoves for shelves, it is necessary to create a visual focus somewhere. This could be a big sofa against the wall, with extending wall-lights either side and a large mirror above. It could be a wall of bookshelves, going right up to the ceiling or a working table with a tall three-panel screen half enclosing it.

Dark colours can look impressive, when boldly and positively handled. A dark gloss finish (Dulux Buckingham gloss) is great in a bathroom, ideally easy to keep clean and makes good camouflage for pipes, cisterns, cupboards you prefer to 'lose'. Softened with lots of white, in different textures, as here, the effect is calm and inviting and not in the least oppressive.

83

This bathroom was not much better than a hole in the wall till painter David Versey got to work on a load of marble washstand tops with his power saw. Now it is positively sybaritic, with sunken bath, marble floor, bench (made from offcuts) and basin, and the odd warming note of stripped and varnished pine.

Due to their hey-presto construction methods, not all these new buildings will take a lot of stuff being suspended from the walls—you have the feeling that screws just poke through into insulation fluff. If studs can be located, I would suspend wall shelves wherever possible, nice scrubbed pine ones on wrought iron brackets, rather than get one of those sad little wall unit arrangements of varnished deal, where every shelf and drawer is just too tiny to be much use. Another device to try, if space allows, is to have pieces of furniture jutting out into the room at right angles to the walls, like a table or desk under the window or low bookcases or hi-fi cabinets each side of unit seating. The object here is to create a room-within-a-room effect, always cosy and attractive, especially at night. Choose unpretentious fabrics, cottons, canvas, poplin with a pleasant, natural texture and jazz things up with fancy cushions, or maybe an old velvet or chenille cover draped over the work table.

The Plainest Jane of a place should be unrecognizable by now. All that remains is to pile on atmosphere, plus one real extravagance, whose main purpose is to quash by its de luxe appearance any lingering sense that this is a deprived area. Old mirrors in gilt frames, ethnic embroideries, sepia photos are all atmosphere creators; in modern rooms, go for bright prints in perspex box frames, a really slick Italian lamp or two, plants. If you collect anything, work out a way of displaying it effectively. Good lighting is essential in a room like this. Try to light necessary areas warmly and leave the rest shadowy. Your extravagance could be anything from a fine kelim, in clear, delicious colours, to a classic modern chair in chrome and leather, but it should *look* as if you had a fling choosing it. If storage is a problem, you might consider splashing out on a helpful piece of furniture—a glass-fronted bookcase, armoire, modern lacquered cabinet. One is usually advised to keep to small unobtrusive pieces in smallish rooms, but I think one fine, substantial piece, preferably a little overscaled, is just what a basic box needs, supplying some of the lacking architectural interest. Old or new, in all this, is up to you and the style you have chosen for your room. Remember, though, that one or two really old things—they could be textiles or lamps, as well as furniture—give off vibrations which new, intrinsically characterless rooms soak up gratefully.

Opposite page: *The razzle-dazzle approach turns a dark basement into a fantastic, luxuriously draped and padded Pandora's box, so colourful and crowded you couldn't care less whether it is night or day outside. Basements are so basic, architecturally, you can have a good deal of fun with them, tenting ceilings, fabric-lining walls, hanging over-scaled pictures—drama, positive thinking is what's needed.*

Kitchens & Bathrooms

There are several good reasons why kitchens and bathrooms are the most thoroughly planned rooms in every house. Equipment for both is expensive, as is installation, so one naturally wants to make the best use of it. Getting the sink and dishwasher lined up with the existing plumbing, and the cooker on an outside wall to simplify extracting steam and smells, can make a noticeable saving on what is usually the most expensive room in any house. Then there is the problem of marrying up the various units, which tend to come in standard sizes, to a room which may not be so conveniently shaped or even possess a single wall that is plumb straight in both directions. Lots of tricky questions about which ways doors open, where the fridge should stand in relation to the sink and cooker, how far forward a hob should be set in the worktop and many more, have to be sorted out on paper very often without the benefit of being able to see it all *in situ*, when obvious mistakes leap to the eye. Some clear-headed people have a gift for working out logical plans taking account of all the factors and difficulties so that everything slots into place without an inch wasted, but they must be exceptional if purpose-built kitchen manufacturers can charge £10,000 upwards for a fitted kitchen. Bathrooms are easier, as a rule, though packing so many bulky items into what is often these days a tiny space, can cause headaches, especially with all the regulations governing outside pipes and drains.

The best way for inexperienced folks to deal with such a complicated bundle of problems is to take it bit by bit. Sink, cooking arrangement (cooker or hob and wall-mounted oven), fridge, dishwasher, are the vital pieces in this chess game. If you already have these, fine, if not you should consult *Which?* or the Good Housekeeping Institute on best buys. Armed with the dimensions of these, take a large piece of chalk and a steel tape and draw them out on the floor of your new kitchen, remembering to allow space at the back for pipes, taps, splashbacks and so on. Standard kitchen wisdom is that cooker, sink and fridge should form a tight triangle in order to reduce time spent running between them, and that there should be relevant storage space near the spot where you need it. So, cupboards for glasses, plates and cutlery should be near the dishwasher or sink, the place for pots and pans near the cooker. Don't at this stage bother too much with all the minor decisions, like where to stack trays, put rolling pins and baking pans, or clean dish towels. The important thing to get right is the basic triangle, and I think make-believe helps here. Rig up some sort of table, if you are going to have a table or island

With plumbing being a speciality of classical Rome, it is only proper that modern bathrooms should pay tribute. The hand-painted classical figures and decorative key border make a very grand bathroom scenario, also highly practical since walls, floor, bath surround are all tiled to match. Another special effect is achieved with the lighting: each figure is individually spotlighted giving life to their static postures.

Above left: *Worn brick floor, warm wood planking, lots of gear standing about on worktops or dangling from hooks on the sloped ceiling — still the most popular look for country or countrified kitchens. The red enamel sink is a surprise (these days porcelain Bristol sinks are making a comeback) but the Aga on the other hand is completely predictable, as are the green wellies.*

Above right: *Like a miniaturized version of the kitchen on the left, this somehow manages to cram all the kitchen status symbols — stripped pine, Aga, fetching kitchen accessories from dried herbs to earthenware storage jars — into a space scarcely large enough to wield a rolling pin. Tiny cooking cockpits like these are in fact highly practical to work in.*

unit, and then mime a few kitchen routines — coming in with the shopping, unpacking it, putting it away. Then there is fetching the stuff for a meal, preparing it, cooking it, getting it to the table. Next clearing away, washing up, putting the crocks and pans away. This can remind you of things you had forgotten, as well as establishing your own pattern of movement in a new context. The more compact your work triangle, the less energy gets wasted moving to and fro. Don't forget, though, that you also have to be able to get to the eating area with your heavy casseroles and frying pans. Allow for the fact that tables need chairs, which take up room too. Manoeuvring round chairs while carrying heavy, hot dishes, is dangerous as well as tiring. I don't think kitchens need to be spacious to be efficient — most people use half the worktop space they provide for — but it is important to site a hob outside the main traffic flow, to prevent racing kids knocking pans off the stove as they charge towards the door.

Having worked out the best arrangement for your big items, the rest should fall into place. Using squared paper, measure and draw out the plan as far as you have it, and then work out how much space is left for all the units, wall cupboards and shelving that you need. People fuss like mad about the correct height for everything but in my experience they often get it wrong by going by the book. If you like to do kitchen chores standing, you need worktops at a different height from those who prefer peeling the potatoes sitting on a stool or at a table. But there is a level between having to crouch and having to stretch, which is the optimum one for storing anything which you make use of regularly in a kitchen. Heavy pots and pans, not often used, can go lower, and everything that one needs only occasionally — from vases to preserving jars — can go higher.

Given a certain amount of planning, a more relaxed, play-it-by-ear approach to the kitchen probably pays off in the end. Old-fashioned kitchens were anything but streamlined, but people functioned well enough in them, and they were often good places to be in, despite their inconveniences. It might be better sometimes to make do with a skeleton kitchen arrangement, testing the lie of the land as it were, instead of rushing headlong into frighten-

ing expenditure which you could regret later. If you simply can't decide what to do with a tricky corner space, just leave it blank for the time being. Even if a standard unit cannot be found to fit, a good joiner will always be able to fix up shelving, even one of those merry-go-round arrangements, when you have decided what you need.

Advertising is always trying to convince us that kitchens should be made of matching interlocking parts, but less streamlined rooms can look more lively, if less tidy, and the food that comes out of them will be just as good. Ace cooks often prefer to have as much as possible of their equipment out on view and within reach, instead of hidden away in cupboards and drawers. One American kitchen has a huge old butcher's block at right angles to the window with a massive post at one end and metal racks above. Large equipment, pots, pans, sieves and colanders hang from butcher's hooks on the metal racks, the beam sprouts so many utensils, hung from nails, that it looks like a small tree and a shelf below the block holds large storage bins for flour and rice as well as heavy kitchen gear. A shelf above the window holds bowls; a shallow rack below saucepan lids; and a magnetic knife rack just below the sill bristles with an armoury of kitchen knives. It has nothing in common with the planning intensive modern kitchens one sees in advertisements, but I could walk in there and prepare a meal without wasting a minute looking for things.

Kitchen Workspace
Worktop space can be extended in a small kitchen by one of the following: a lift-up flap which folds against the wall; a board which slides out above a set of drawers; a detachable cover to fit over the sink; a ceramic hob.

Ideal worktop heights vary: kneading dough is best done at table height; chopping and prep-aration at just below elbow height; whisking and mixing are less tiring done sitting down—an adjustable stool is a great boon in the kitchen.

Deep drawers on rollers are practical for low level storage; and a revolving unit makes wasted corner space useful and accessible.

Kitchens, especially if one eats in them too, should be friendly and attractive places, as well as practical ones. There is a welcome move back to natural surfaces—wood, tiles, brick—and away from laminates and vinyl. Make sure, if you are investing in wooden worktops, that the wood is tough enough to take endless mopping and chopping—having to use a separate chopping board on wooden worktops seems superogatory. Tiled worktops are sensible if the tiles are thick, solid ones which can take heavy things banged down on them. Stainless steel is still a splendid material, especially if you can afford to take it right over an entire worktop, as well as sinks and draining boards. It has a no-nonsense, restaurant-kitchen practicality which puts a cook at ease. Mixed with natural materials like tiles and wood, it need not look clinical. Splashbacks can be tiled, mirror, wood or slate. Remember to get plenty of power points set into them, spaced so that one person trying to make tea from the electric kettle isn't under the feet of another feeding ingredients into the food processor. Sliding doors on units take up less space but, unless their design is brilliant, there is often an inaccessible dead space somewhere in the middle. Some deep drawers, wide enough to take rolling pins, as well as dish towels and table mats are a help, but you don't need stacks of them. Recessed toe space under units is very practical, allowing you to stand up close to the task in hand. Stacking crockery, glasses and storage jars on shallow open shelves up one wall is a practical, cheap storage solution which works well in a small galley-type kitchen, but everything, including the shelves, will need much more cleaning to get rid of that sticky kitchen fall-out.

Now this is a good space, and so it should be since both owners—Nick Waites and Caroline Lwin, seen here with baby May—are very much into architecture. The glazed roof section is a great way of admitting light. Note the way the studded plastic flooring curves up to meet the wall units, makes cleaning easier and gives a streamlined look.

Crisp as graph paper, the beautifully precise alignment of ceramic tiles for floor and splashback in a sophisticated high-tech kitchen where the thought-out detailing and expensive equipment reinforces my theory that the high-tech look needs care and money to come across. There is a nice, almost Japanese game of contrasting texture and pattern between the chair caning and the biscuit shaped tiles. Notice how a flash of red galvanizes in a low key colour scheme.

Spend some time choosing sensible taps, with handles that are easy to grip and turn, and a mixer spout that projects far enough to avoid water splashing back all over the place. Taps need a wider ledge to sit in than they usually get, plus some easily wiped form of splashback. Finally, stop to check out the practicalities of every kitchen item before the salesgirl can chat you into thinking you can't live without it. A girl I know bought her house largely on the strength of its pretty kitchen, with coloured enamelled sink instead of stainless steel. It wasn't till she cooked her first Sunday roast that she discovered her pretty sink was too small to take a standard baking tin.

The most practical bathroom is probably the best if a lot of people use it. The ideal would be one of those all-marble numbers one finds in Spain, where marble is cheaper, or a really sleek high-tech effort, tiled throughout. It would have a heated towel rail, but not one so hot or so awkwardly placed that it takes a strip off your backside if you are foolish enough to back into it. An airing cupboard is useful though, if the hot-water tank can be found a home somewhere else without further complicating the plumbing, there may be handier spots to locate one. Dressing-tables are supposed to be returning to favour, but I find most women still use the bathroom mirror for make-up purposes, which means a place must be found for all those jars, bottles, powder boxes, lipsticks and hair curlers. Where room permits, setting a basin into an old-fashioned sideboard, or desk, is neat because it gives storage space and plenty of surface area *en suite*, as well as allowing you to slide your feet under the kneehole. Antique bathroom fittings are understandably popular,

being handsome, generously scaled and nice to handle but *aficionados* should be warned that plumbing them in can be a shock to a chap used to standard modern fittings and improvisation can lead to nasty surprises. My weakness for this sort of thing means I have a basin without a proper grid over the plug hole so bottle caps falling in disappear and block the waste pipe. My beautiful antique brass taps, with Hot and Cold on their porcelain tops, have a horrid disparity of water pressure, so that hot jets out in a scalding stream while cold meanly dribbles. These are some of the problems that can arise when one tries to attach antique fittings to modern parts. On the other hand, if you stick to a popular colour like white, it is certainly cheaper to collect bathroom fixtures in diverse places, like street markets or architectural salvage stores like Lassco (the London Architectural Salvage & Supply Company) in Shoreditch, which not so long ago thronged with the grandest alabaster fittings from the Savoy Hotel.

A pretty, cheery-looking bathroom, with some concessions to comfort, like carpeted floor, nice colours and a bookshelf, is a definite morale booster on cold, dark mornings. Many existing bathrooms inherited with old flats, are hell holes to look at—dank, dark and draped with exposed piping. Paint is the answer here. You can paint everything a good, strong colour, like gauloise blue or bright green (pipes and all) and introduce the comfort with thick, large towels, a chair to perch on while cutting toenails or drying the feet, some pictures. Or you can go to town on fake glamour, sponging everything including pipes and ceiling and any woodwork to look like pinky marble, filling corners with plants (real ones enjoy bathroom damp and warmth, but fakes are quite acceptable), and keeping soap in large seashells. Boxing the entire bath in with trellis (the plastic kind sold in sheets at DIY centres), to resemble a summerhouse or gazebo, is currently fashionable—an extra light over the bath will be necessary.

Not a few currently fashionable notions in this pretty little bathroom—lace curtains, lace inspired stencils on bath surround, old-time bath fittings like brass taps, kitsch dancer posing in silhouette and one of those ubiquitous shaped glass mirrors, upside down.

Opposite page: *A fairly amazing venue for a bathroom, slotted in under the massive roof beams of an Oxfordshire converted barn and the decor makes the most of it with its lavish use of printed fabric, polished brass on the fireplace (ritzy touch that). Tall mirrors expand the space as well as disguising doors to clothes cupboards.*

Simple Storage

What might be called the inertia factor is probably the determining thing in whether a storage system works or doesn't. Some people can maintain order and neatness with one cupboard, a couple of shelves, and a trunk under the bed. Others will spill chaotically out of rooms crammed with cupboards, chests and shelving in houses generously provisioned with attic and cellar space, not to mention that sad, musty little place called a boxroom. Putting things away needs to be made as easy as wink for most people, families especially. The moment hanging up coats, putting books back or getting dirty clothes to the wash room involves thought and extra effort, there is a tendency for inertia to prevail and things just accumulate in heaps where they are. I have yet to see a kitchen dresser, for instance, which was not half obliterated by the flotsam and jetsam of daily life, socks needing mending, invitations, unopened buff envelopes, library books, a hairbrush, at least one bag, a few toy cars, a flute.

Storage space is essential, if life is to have any sense of peace, calm and order about it. But it only works if it is used routinely and it will only be used like that if it is conveniently sited, easy to get at and well lit. You can hardly spend too long anticipating the problems that might arise in using a particular cupboard. For instance, I have some cupboards filling in space under the stairs which have doors that do not come right down to the floor. Instead the cupboard frame continues round below, vaguely matching up with the skirting elsewhere (and incidentally simplifying the joinery for the carpenter who made them because the doors did not need a stop to close against). The lower section of this cupboard space is used for vacuum cleaners, suitcases and sewing-machines. The problem is that because of the lintel, lifting these things in and out is a bore and an effort and, no doubt, dreadful for the vertebrae. I don't have to tell you that once out, the contents are rarely returned to base. Another frequent boob is the high up cupboard, supposed to be good for storing winter woollies through the summer, or tennis gear through the winter. You can bet your life, unless a sturdy set of steps is to hand, they will remain empty, or once filled up, quite forgotten.

Being one of those perverse beings, an untidy person who craves order, I have given much thought to the psychology of storage. How amazing, for example, the propriety of medieval rooms whose entire storage consisted of a heavy oak coffer at the foot of the bed, and possibly some sort of crude armoire standing against a wall. Oak chests or painted bridal chests in Early

Converting a loft into a bedroom need not mean losing all that useful storage space when the bed is raised up on a purpose-built platform, with doors leading to a capacious cupboard below. More wall cupboards and a couple of bookshelves make this a snug place to retreat to, with a cabin feel to it. Woodwork suggestion: Dulux Pine Interior Varnish.

American style are handsome objects into which no end of blankets, linen and hand-stitched petticoats can fit. But they also have inviting solid lids on which people put books, plants and television sets so that extracting an extra blanket for the guest room bed becomes something of a chore. Everything must be taken off the top, a lamp brought nearer, the contents investigated, layer by layer, then the whole process repeated in reverse.

Contrary to popular opinion I think storage only becomes a pressing problem when there are several of you, irrespective of the size of the place. One, even two, people can make out nicely in a tiny flat, because they have the leisure to plan, to pack unseasonal clothes in labelled boxes or bags and the incentive to stash them away tidily, out of sight. They are more in control of their lives. Even if they aren't, one's own mess is tolerable, it is other people's which is so offensive. Small flat dwellers probably already know all the wheezes, like drawers under beds (you can buy them like that now), false ceilings in bathrooms creating a tiny boxroom, seating which lifts up, shelving which is strung together by cords but is strong enough to take a full-grown man recumbent—for flats where drilling and plugging walls is frowned upon. Shops are full of attractive things like wall-pockets to stuff knitting or stationery in, and bright plastic boxes of drawers for all your odds and ends. I think curtains hung across alcoves or corners of rooms, make pleasingly bohemian and cheap places to hide your clothes, unless they are so decorative you prefer to make a feature of them, with a sort of clothes tree. What no one much wants to do, if they don't own the place, is to spend money putting in cupboards. Everything needs to be free standing, self supporting and movable.

Families can just about be contained in the average two or three bed-roomed house or flat, with a garage, shed or outside repository for prams, bikes and gardening gear. When I see magazine articles (usually in French magazines) about this trendy couple, he in the media, she a designer, with two children, all packed together into an ingeniously sub-divided one-room apart-ment in some posh *quartier*, I grit my teeth in sympathy. That may be bliss for *jeunes amoureux* but the torments of family life under such conditions hardly bears thinking about.

Self Assembly Furniture
Self-assembly furniture comes up with inventive solutions to packing a lot into a small space—a raised platform bed over a desk recess and a small wardrobe costs less than £150—much cheaper than paying a good carpenter to make it up for you. And you can take it with you when you move.

THE ATMOSPHERE

The Spirit of Place

Atmosphere in a place is like charm in a person, instantly felt and recognized but hard to nail down with words. Like charm, too, it exerts a spell. Entering a place without atmosphere is a zero experience but, when you go into an atmospheric room, vibrations are exchanged, your awareness is tuned up, the *genius loci*—the spirit of the place—is transmitting and this can be felt almost physically. Not all atmospheres are beneficent, or exorcists would not be in business, but a good atmosphere is as reassuring, even to strangers, as a friendly hug. The good feeling about a place remains in one's mind after the details of decor and furnishings are forgotten. Atmosphere has to do with a place feeling 'real', which is something beyond the way it looks, though colours and textures play a part in establishing a room's personality. Finally, I think, atmosphere stems from people, an emanation of individual lives stored up in the very fabric of a building, which is why almost all ancient buildings give off such a powerful charge.

Pinpointing the atmospheric is elusive and decorators who have a reputation for knowing how to infuse this mysterious quality into their clients' homes are very much in demand, though they would be the first to admit that without some participation by the clients themselves, an engagement with the colours, fabrics, arrangement of things, the results can be sadly disappointing, like a red rose with no scent. It is one of the little ironies of fashion that atmosphere, which is just about the one element money cannot furnish a place with, is currently the most coveted asset. 'Make me a place that looks as if it had always been that way,' is the cry, 'different, interesting, *real*.' A talented decorator can whistle up the effect of atmosphere, create mood, but after that it is up to the people who live there to bring it to life, adding, enriching.

Aids to atmosphere might include any, or indeed all, of the following.

Poetic colour—What decorators call 'dirty colours' (raw umber mixed into almost any colour dirties it appealingly) give a gentle, moody look to a place. If you prefer warmth to wistfulness, paint walls a pinky brown (Dulux Rosetan maybe) and rag it over with a rich red glaze. Red is a tricky decorating colour, but a trump card if you enjoy it and want a positive-looking environment. Any distressed paint finish helps inject atmosphere because it looks softer, more suggestive, opened-out rather than walled-in. Painting everything one colour in a room (except the ceiling) walls, woodwork, shelves as in my own blue study (see page 98), makes a place look and feel peaceful, nurturing.

Bare floors—Wooden floors—bare, not shabby but stained green or red and waxed over, with a few rugs for softening, give surprising character to a room. Painted, then stencilled, or chequered and varnished, they look good too, a touch historical. If you are stuck with mottled vinyl tiles, cover them up with matting.

Light—A gentle, diffused light by day, a soft, flickering light by night is a potent atmosphere creator. Old lace curtains or new lace curtains steeped in strong tea for a parchment shade, soften the light romantically, and long louvred shutters cast painterly shadows on a sunny day. Use peachy-coloured lampshades, with an uplighter hidden behind plants or a chair to make dramatic silhouettes. If there is a fireplace, use it—fire light is the most atmospheric kind there is. After that, of course, there comes candlelight.

Scents—Bowls of pot-pourri, burning logs, scented candles, lavender heaped in bowls, give a room soul.

Books—You can't have too many, but they must be read.

Personal things—Mementoes, photos, pinboards, needlework in progress.

Mirrors—Easy magic, but choose them old, mottled, pewtery, for preference. Or use sheet mirror on walls and drape it, so the reflection is glimpsed, like a window.

Colour Coding

Knowing how to make colour work for you is at least half the secret of decorating with style, especially if you are trying to make a big effect with very little cash. If your colours are good—by which I mean pleasing in themselves and suited to the rooms—your place will look special even if the furniture is junk, the carpet is going bald and the springs are dropping out of the sofa. Colour clothes a room. It also disguises. Use it to open up a small room, brighten a gloomy one, soften a raw new box. More specifically, it can be used to 'lose' ugly fittings, like tangles of pipes.

There are many ways of introducing colour to your home, but the cheapest and, in many ways, most satisfactory is with paint. The beauty of paint be it on walls, ceilings, floors, woodwork, even furniture is that if things don't quite turn out as you had expected—which happens to all of us now and then—the results can be corrected or modified relatively easily. Transparent glazes, used in one of the fashionable decorative finishes (stippled, ragged, sponged) go on as fast and easily as varnish and can be used to soften, cool down or boost the ground colour as the case may be (see pages 156–165). Playing about with coloured glazes and decorative finishes is one of the best ways to strengthen your own colour sense.

Provide yourself with a tin of scumble glaze (see Paint Types chart, pages 156–157) and some tubes of artists' oil paints (or cheaper universal stainers, as sold in DIY and trade shops) and mess about with these for an hour or two, trying different combinations over your existing colour (mistakes can be wiped off easily with a rag damped with white spirit). Don't be afraid of trying unexpected colour mixes or two colours on top of a third—this sort of colour building creates painterly effects which can be quite beautiful. Do, on the other hand, go slowly and try to make notes of what you are using so that if you decide to steam ahead with sludge green over gauloise blue, or brick pink over duck egg blue, you have the formula to hand. Getting it right is largely a matter of instinct—learn to trust the hunch that comes to you and learn to trust your eye. Brush, rag or sponge your glaze over a sizeable patch of wall (use painted boards if you are nervous of getting it off completely or do it in a spot behind a large piece of furniture), stand back, walk around, move bits of furniture or coloured cushions against it to gauge the effect but, whatever you do, don't rush your decisions. All the most talented designers feel their way into a colour scheme, step by step, leaving as many options open as possible for as long as possible.

People are always insisting that blue is a cold colour but this blue, though moody and light absorbing—it needs twice the wattage at night—is a warm and pensive shade, ideal for a study. I arrived at it by mixing ultramarine and burnt umber powder colours, diluted in water, into a standard Dulux Matchmaker Lakestone vinyl matt emulsion. I mixed up the same shade in silthane silk for the woodwork. The frieze—hand-painted detail and stencils—was taken from an Indian bedcover motif.

Mixing Your Own Colours
Beginners should buy a basic range of universal stainers which are cheaper than artists' quality colours. As an exercise, try mixing them to match paper or fabric in colours you like. For a strong but thundery blue, for instance, put a dab of blue stainer on a white plate, then small dots of yellow, umber, black and red round the edge. With your fingers or a brush, mix a little of each in turn with the basic blue and rub on to white paper to gauge the effect. Now intermix, but tentatively—a strong, thundery blue would probably need blue, burnt umber and a little red. Don't automatically add black to a colour to darken it—it might eclipse it altogether. This is basic colour training and what you learn can be applied to mixing up paints on a larger scale.

Opposite page: *These red drag-painted walls would not win any prizes for technique, but the red—warm, soft without being glaring—illustrates how successfully this difficult colour can be achieved by distressing a transparent glaze in one shade of red over a plain matt coat of paint in another shade of red. The base coat was a silk vinyl in a dull brick pink (Dulux Sweetgale) over which was dragged a glaze tinted a ripe strawberry red. A similar red is picked up in the handwoven chenille upholstery.*

This approach gives results as different from the safe formula approach beloved of DIY problem pages and lazy decorators as a rich and subtle painting is from a screen print. Safe formulas are useful at times, but there is no way in which a room scheme thought up in your head or put together from swatches and colour samples is going to give the same sense of gradual unfolding, of unexpected treats and harmonies, which distinguishes a room that has been lovingly brooded over and gradually pieced together, without plan perhaps but with a responsive eye and open mind.

Whichever colour you are deciding about—walls, curtains, carpet, furnishings—group together all the other shades in the room and then try a series of different possible colours with them, using sheets of coloured paper, frocks, anything large enough to give some idea of how the colours will eventually interact. I collect odd lengths of fabric in flea markets in the sort of colours I like to use and, while these are waiting to be made up into cushions or chair covers, they come in useful for providing colour ideas while I am making up my mind. One of the mysteries of colour is that any new colour you introduce into an existing setting tends to alter the relationship of the colours already there—ask any painter. Often there may be half a dozen colours which would 'go' with what you have, but in that lot there may be one or a particular shade of one, which wakes up the existing scheme and that is the colour you are searching for. When you have found the colour, you still have to think about texture and light. A pink that sets your teeth on edge in a shiny fabric could be deliciously vivid in matt cotton. Conversely a russet which glows in a silky textured velvet might look frowsty in a fabric which gave the colour without the shine. The amount of light and the way it falls also affects colour. A colour which would look terrific covering a chair in one corner of a room might be too much altogether used for curtains at all the windows.

I never believe people who tell me they have no colour sense. Nearly everyone is drawn strongly, probably unconsciously, to one or two colours in preference to all the rest. These are the colours one tends to wear or look twice at when shopping for fabrics, china, in fact, virtually anything. If you look at your clothes hanging in a cupboard some sort of colour theme usually emerges. Mine inclines towards all the warm, earthy colours, from tawny yellow right through to terracotta, while someone else might be just as irresistibly drawn by cool, sharp turquoise blues, light greens, cold mauves. Only children probably have one absolutely top favourite colour; adult preferences tend to be for groups which harmonize together. This could be something you do without realizing it. Try browsing through a selection of dress or furnishing fabrics or Indian cotton prints and choose the ones which just appeal to you the most, in themselves, as colours. Usually you will find that it is not just yellow, say, which grabs your attention but yellow balanced by a particular faded mauve or vivid green. In other words, it is not one but a conjunction of several colours which most affects you. By analysing these colour combinations in some detail, in a successful example, you often come across some surprises.

For instance, liking warm colours as I do, I have always found oriental rugs based on a particular faded red irresistible. Looking at them over the years has provided me with a whole range of colours which combine happily, in varying proportions, with the basic red—slate blue, cerulean blue, a light apple green, straw yellow, black, washed-out mauve, dirty pink. Unconsciously, I find myself collecting old fabrics and prints in these colours, and most of the rooms I plan use some or all of these colours, somewhere. This doesn't mean that I only have faded red rooms with touches of blue and green—one can play these colour combinations many ways, taking blue as the main colour one time, dirty pink another. But I do have at the back of my

Monochrome rooms, like this exercise in pale grey-blue (Dulux Billow vinyl matt) and white are reposeful, un-demanding. This is an introverted sort of room, reticent, a better place to listen to music than hold a party.

mind a mental image of how it will look one day, which I am quietly working towards. This kind of room, the painterly atmospheric room, is never finished, at least not where its maker is concerned. Once you are tuned in to a rich colour mix, you will find yourself continually adding to it. Rugs happen to provide my colour inspiration but if you look about you, in shops, museums, stately homes or magazines, you will find something to suit your own colour preferences. For sharp, sophisticated colours—vivid yellow, peacock blue, cerise, emerald green—look at Chinese embroideries, or eighteenth-century painted porcelain. For cool subtle combinations of neutrals and soft pebble shades, I would consult Japanese and Korean pottery, heathery tweeds and hand-woven rugs. Muted pastels are beautifully combined in just about any packet of pot-pourri or dried flowers. Once one learns to enjoy colour as a delicious extra dimension, instead of backing off nervously as if it were an esoteric mystery, inspiration turns up everywhere and the more you look the more you see.

This is an approach to colour which is both flexible and safe—in the sense that if you go slowly you make no big, expensive mistakes. If you want to test a daring idea, do it on a small scale—buy some flowers in that colour or cover a cushion or two, then consider the effect, live with it a while, imagine it scaled up or down, in a different texture, maybe broken up by a printed design, with other colours on top of it (like a divan piled with cushions or walls bordered or powdered with stencils), with the furniture shifted round, with the electric light on. Think of it as a game, but a creative one.

Believing that people should live with the colours that make them happiest and that this is something they can work out only for themselves, I am sceptical about colour prescriptions and formulas. On the other hand, working with colours and constantly observing what other people do with them, I have picked up some useful tips and suggestions.

VIVID COLOURS

Vivid colours need firm handling. Rooms can take vivid walls if: you plan to cover most of the wall surface with pictures, prints or mementoes; you use a distressed paint finish, or tone on tone printed wallpaper; or you parry the intensity of a large area of bright colour by using other colours of similar intensity with it. The last approach is risky, of course, but can look wonderfully exciting—think of Matisse. Candida Lycett-Green has painted rooms in her country house in orangey-red (meant to be tomato, but came out more carrot), Granny Smith green, strong cobalt blue—all of them, anything but traditional country house colours. But, having established the visual zap, she then covers the walls with pictures, prints, photos and mirrors, uses bold and colourful prints for curtains, chair and table covers, slings in a completely personal mix of old things, pretty things, bright spots of different colour (yellow roses in a pink jug) and nicely elaborate bits of charming Victoriana like papier mâché inlaid with mother of pearl and needlework cushions. The carrotty room has a vivid pink sofa and two cherry and white checked gingham chair covers—against the rules, but dashingly successful. To do a Candida you need the confidence and the gear. Lacking these, the thing to do if you want positive, bright colours around you, is to go for a tone on tone version—vivid blue made up of two shades of blue, red on red, or green on green. Look for a wallpaper (Morris, Voysey did lovely ones on these lines) or get it more cheaply by using two paint shades superimposed, dragging or stippling or sponging to let both shades mingle.

RED

Red should always be distressed. Grand houses can sometimes take a strong pure red because there is usually a lot going on visually, be it cornices, dado rails, plaster ornaments, panelled effects, chequered marble floors, to dilute the effect. The rest of us have to be more subtle if we are not to feel we are living in a furnace. Go for dull, dirty or complicated reds and put one sort on top of another for a soft rich glow that does not hurt the eye. I would drag-paint a deep brown red over a brick pink, a slightly bluish red over a slightly yellowish one. Then drag a greyish or buff glaze over all the white-painted woodwork to soften the contrast. Mongrelly reds like these have great character and warmth and are easy to live with—perfect for a smallish town room without too much natural light and ideal on cold evenings. The Matisse painting of a red dining-room is a lesson to us all on handling red.

WARM COLOURS

Yellows, apricots and certain pinks are the easiest warm colours to use successfully. Everyone likes them, though they can be cloying and sugary if you don't mix in some strong, dull, dark colour for muscle like black, spinach green, slate blue or that dark brownish red the colour of oxblood shoe polish. Apricot and yellow ragged or sponged over white is instant sunshine, charming for country cottages. Strong yellow, like cadmium, with a faint tinge of green is a magnificent colour for dark, narrow front halls. Varnish it for shine and depth (for shine, use varnish over a matt colour, it looks softer and richer than gloss paint) and collect black and white engravings and mezzotints to hang everywhere. These colours combine well with other pastels, à la Tricia Guild, but note that her best prints usually include something bitter,

Colour Building
Practice in mixing colours means you can start with your can of commercial paint and modify it by adding a little of this or that to get the precise shade you want. Start with a colour close to the one you want, but paler.

For warm pinks and apricots, burnt sienna, raw sienna plus white (in varying amounts) give clear sunny colours. Burnt sienna plus small amounts of alizarin, vermillion, one of the warm reds (Venetian, Indian red or red oxide—use these sparingly as they are powerful tints) and maybe a little raw or burnt umber, or cobalt blue, will give a great range of reds of an earthy character. Bluer reds should start from alizarin and have the warmer shades added gradually.

Adding raw or burnt umber to blues, pale or dark, makes them more interesting. Delicious duck egg blues are obtained by adding varying amounts of white to cerulean, with a little chrome yellow and raw umber.

Chrome yellow and black make a good eighteenth-century drab green, to which white gives a mustardy shade. Raw umber and Paynes grey with a little raw sienna in white gives a soft, warm grey, excellent for woodwork as a foil to glazed or papered walls.

Keep to the chrome yellows (plus a hint of umber or a fleck of red) for sharp, sophisticated yellow. Ochre and raw sienna with white give creamier shades, verging on buff.

khaki, or purple-blue, to offset so much sweetness. Peachy pinks, particularly, can be sickly in excess, needing cooling down with watery blues and mauves and sharpening with khaki, ginger, lime green. The pink I like best is much darker, and colder, almost a cool light red. One finds it in the murals at Pompeii. With slightly greyed woodwork, it is an exciting colour to use in a semi-formal, Georgian-style living- or dining-room.

QUIET, COOL COLOURS

The first choice of most men (though not designers), these include the tranquil greyed pastels, grey-blue, grey-green, grey-buff and brown in the lighter tones. They are the least demanding of all colours, but they need polished handling if they are not to look glum. I see them as background colours and backgrounds need foregrounds—plenty of texture, warmly polished wood, old gilding, leather, plus chunks of warm but subdued colour in fabrics, rugs and pictures. Built-in texture always looks amazingly sophisticated in these colours—walls covered with grey flannel or suede-effect, snuff-coloured paper or a textured wall covering in colour and texture resembling sea-grass. Shabbiness or meagreness is to be avoided; a nicely worn-in effect is good with warm colours, dark colours, but these just look seedy if you fill the room up with battered armchairs, beat-up rugs, limp curtains or if the actual wall surfaces are stained or scuffed.

Deeper versions of these Quakerish colours can look highly distinguished—bilberry blue, sepia brown, charcoal grey, the cold greens—all to me, pensive shades, ideally suited to studies, masculine living-rooms, bedrooms. I like them warmed up with lots of mahogany, quiet overall printed fabrics (some of the monochrome Morris prints) a fur rug or two, leather chairs. Discarding the gentlemanly image, they can also take happily to the wilder flights of ethnic tat, Indian embroideries, calico prints, vividly striped rugs draped over chairs and sofas, polished brass or copper. It takes courage to paint or paper a light-coloured room a positively dark hue, but it is a particularly effective way of giving a not-very-special room a feeling of mystery and character. Paradoxically, dark, dim hallways and rooms sometimes come into their own if, instead of trying to go for lightness and brightness, you decide to make a virtue of necessity, go for a rich dark colour and then hang as many mirrors, pictures and prints as you can lay hands on.

MONOCHROME OR NO-COLOUR ROOMS

In decorating it is hard to find anything new. The pale, one-colour rooms currently creeping back into fashion are throwbacks to the all-white rooms made fashionable in the Thirties by the formidable Syrie Maugham, wife of Somerset for a brief turbulent spell (see pages 11–12). Since the Thirties many designers and decorators have played about with the monochrome theme and, properly done, it always works. But anyone tempted to follow suit should be prepared to give it some thought and effort. Drastically simplified effects like these lay extra emphasis on detail—paintwork should be immaculate, smooth, walls flawlessly painted or papered, furnishings pristine, dustless and spotless. Otherwise it just looks as if you had ducked out of the colour problem and come up with a half-hearted alternative. Cut-price versions, I think, are both possible and attractive—calico and canvas instead of linen or silk, painted floors instead of best grade Wilton carpet, plastic instead of lacquer, but it needs to be done with real conviction and, if possible, it should always incorporate one casually handled noble material—a marble fireplace, stone-flagged floor, a suede-covered chair.

The more texture you can introduce, while keeping to the chosen one-colour look, the richer and more sophisticated the effect. An off-white or cream-coloured room might be rag-rolled or ragged (ultra-sophisticated

What with What?
The works of painters like Matisse, Bonnard, Dufy are packed with a lifetime's wisdom in handling and positioning colour. Anyone can think of a safe colour combination using just two or three shades, but artists can help you find the unexpected flash of cerise pink, ultramarine, chrome yellow or violet which gives that safe scheme life. Don't forget black, either. Michael Astor used to say that a good room like a good painting needed some black somewhere— and he was right. Look at paintings by Manet or Degas.

Colour is so subjective that you must work out your own preferences in the end—but here are a few thoughts on mixtures I have seen and liked: strong yellow and strong blue with some terracotta and sap green; sharp yellow and washy violet with a dark bitter red, like ox blood; apricot and acid pink with drab, ultramarine and vermilion; sludge green, watery azure, coral, coffee brown and black.

Colour schemes go awry most often if you keep to too *few* colours, because then the precise tone and texture matter so much. People *will* put together olive green and golden yellow, thinking of daffodils or corn fields and forgetting that Nature includes brown soil, blue sky, red poppies, mauve columbine, pink dog roses . . .

104

One-colour kitchens (this one is Dulux Bluebell White vinyl silk) like these have a sort of hygienic chic which some people find a great deal more reassuring than all those homely surfaces like waxed pine, scrubbed bricks, which presumably harbour a million bugs, moulds, whatever. The bonus of such parsimonious use of colour is that one tomato, or a bowl of oranges, sings out like a blast of trumpets in contrast.

finishes, these) in tone on tone, parchment over off-white for instance, which gives a cool marbly look with great depth. Then paint floorboards shiny broken white, giving several coats of eggshell varnish for protection and to deepen the shine. Over this go white fur rugs or Indian cream wool rugs. Slip-covers and curtains could be canvas or duck, a bit tailored looking—both materials washable which is vital if the elegant look is to be kept up. Cushion covers might be quilted satin, or creamy corduroy (incidentally, corduroy looks great for upholstery, sportier than velvet and cheaper). Lampshades can be pleated parchment, plain white cotton or basketwork which gives a kindly broken light. Alternatively, white industrial metal shades low hung over areas where you want direct light (beside sofas, over a desk, bookcase or table) but used with globe bulbs which give the softest diffused light. Use cheap carpet fringe (off-white, or string colour) on curtains. Make ruched blinds from plain calico to diffuse natural light if you have very large windows—so much paleness can be glaring, if the outside light isn't filtered—or hang white cotton roller blinds or the palest pinoleum. Having set the cool pale mono-chrome look, you can have fun adding juicy bits and pieces to enrich the effect.

White on white is particularly good for bedrooms because these get used less often and so stay fresher longer. It also gives great scope for using up all the old laces and linens which can still be found at jumble sales and market stalls. Lavishly used, two or three cloths draped over tables, swags of lace round the bed, crocheted doilies on the furniture (or stitched into cushion covers), look absurdly romantic and luxurious, especially in a creamy pale setting. Wicker chairs sprayed off-white and varnished are the obvious seating solution, with cushions covered in any scraps you may be hoarding.

Making Your Bed

Since we spend a third of our lives in them—probably more now that television and video-watching in bedrooms is becoming a popular way to unwind—it is rather surprising that beds do not get more attention when people decorate their sleeping quarters. They are such dull-looking objects, most of them, and yet so easy to dramatize. Dressing up a bed makes it look more inviting and luxurious as well as giving an integrated look to the whole room if you do it cleverly.

DIVANS

Single beds pushed up against the wall or into a corner look cosier and oriental if you run a hanging of some sort along the wall behind. A length of velvet or richly printed cotton looks good but it is best to back any floppy fabric on to canvas or, alternatively, staple it taut. Old rugs look even better, as do embroideries or patchwork—this is a striking way of using the good bits of an old patchwork quilt, like the Victorian silk ones which are too fragile to handle. If you can edge the wall-hanging with old braid, so much the better, it will look more finished. Stack cushions up against the wall cover, hang pictures above and a modest bed has acquired presence.

Beds in cupboards are an ancient idea, popular in cold countries where they needed to cut out draughts. Enclosing beds in some way, with fabric if panelling seems too extravagant, can look charming, creating a room within a room. A single bed pushed up sideways against the wall could have curtains running on ceiling tracks at each end. Alternatively, a canopy effect could start at the ceiling, then swoop down each side with long metal brackets covered to match the drapes and firmly screwed to the back wall to support them. More stapled-on fabric hides the supports and gives a tented look. Use yet more of the same fabric to cover the base.

STANDARD BEDS

Conventional beds tend to have headboards and footboards. If yours is polished brass, or sandblasted iron, it will be wonderful enough already, especially if you skirt it lavishly all round between the frame and the floor—use a cheap fabric, like calico, but generously, and maybe stitch coarse lace around the hem.

Wooden bed ends can, of course, be painted to blend with the room, preferably with one of the decorative finishes, like stippling. But padding out and covering them both with one of the room fabrics is more comfortable

An interesting bedroom scheme this, stopping just short of freakiness with its lavish use of black marbled paintwork against walls of palest pink (Dulux Daydream vinyl matt for example). It reminds me of Tilly Losch's famous, mildly decadent pink-and-black bathroom of the Thirties, though this has unmistakably Eighties detail like the pink tubular bedframe and halogen lamp.

A fine rosewood bateau bed is the star of this plain but pretty bedroom in early nineteenth-century style, its rich graining set off by a coverlet and draped canopy of discreetly printed cotton. Note how the tiny formal arrangements of black framed miniatures and prints are picked up by the 'print room' treatment of the grey-painted landing—black and white reproduction prints framed in borders cut from Times Court Circulars, *pasted direct to walls.*

and feels more luxurious. With a staple gun it takes only minutes. First staple $\frac{3}{4}$ inch (19 mm) foam wadding over the wood, pulling it taut around any mouldings. Pad both sides of each fabric panel—it only uses a scrap more foam and looks ten times better. If you have any spare calico or sheeting make an undercover before stapling on the final fabric. It will keep your wadding firmly in place and give a sleek look. You will need a toning braid, ribbon or other trimming to hide the staples, at least on the footboard. Bed-heads with square posts either side of a flat board can still be covered, and padded, but treat the posts separately, padding and stapling them first as shown in the drawing and then turning in the raw edges of the final cover before stapling on top as shown. Stick braid on top.

The fabric covering could match the curtains or bedcover. Having got this far, it is relatively simple to pile on the glamour with a gathered panel of one of the two fabrics hung from a rod—this makes it look more finished, but you could use staples—fixed to the top of the wall behind the bed. If you are using a rod with decorative finials, simply stitch a tubular opening near the top of this panel and slip the rod through it, arranging the gathers evenly. This simple treatment would suit any decor, modern or period, as it looks neither feminine nor theatrical.

If you *do* want your bed to look theatrical or feminine, you could try a half-tester arrangement, with half curtains cascading from a round or boxy pelmet fixed securely to the wall. This is elegant and not difficult to do with the staple gun. (To clean or wash stapled hangings, incidentally, simply prise out the staples and fix them back later.) The pelmet or tester can be covered

with the same or a contrasting fabric inside and out. All sorts of odd finds lend themselves to conversion for testers—picture frames, the detachable top cornice of cupboards, even a drawer covered and turned upside down before being screwed to the wall. Depending on what sort of wall it is going on, you may be able to screw straight into studs behind, or you might have to use brackets for extra strength, even toggle bolts. Make sure it is absolutely rigid and solid because gathered fabric can be heavy and no one wants to be brained in their sleep! Dressed-up beds should be fantastic, so don't be afraid to experiment with different effects before making up your mind. Hangings could be cotton lace, or printed or plain cotton, or both, using the plain cotton as outer curtains and the print inside. Catch the edges together with invisible stitches or bind with braid or a ruffle. The sides can be pulled out and caught back on decorative finials or with a heavy tassel on a cord loop.

Cottage charm, honest as apple pie, its patchwork quilt, simple pine furniture, a suitably artless foil to the Beatrix Potter landscape outside.

FOUR-POSTERS OR NEARLY

This is the supreme bed, only possible perhaps in a room with a high ceiling and enough floor space to give it pride of place and still leave room for other furniture. Cheat four-posters, however, made by running curtains from a ceiling track, give much the same effect a great deal more cheaply and undemandingly, while taking advantage of a lower ceiling. The most solid and satisfactory way to do this is to screw wooden moulding into the ceiling and either fix curtain tracks inside it (this is best if they will need frequent taking down and laundering) or staple curtains directly into the inside of the moulding. Tenting in the top completes the illusion.

Four-posters, the real sort with posts, are not prodigiously difficult feats of carpentry; the chief problem encountered is making them quite rigid, braced in such a way that they won't sway. Turned posts in various woods—deal for painting, mahogany for polishing up—can be bought from specialists in mouldings or decorative woodwork and cost approximately £25 each, unfinished.

If you already own a four-poster, there are many ways of dressing it. Eighteenth-century four-posters usually had two sets of curtains and valances. one for winter and one for summer. As a rule the well-dressed four-poster has an outer and inner set, one in a lighter, softer fabric than the other. I made my inner curtains from the same striped shirting that I used to cover walls and quilt curtains.

On the other hand, they can be left flimsy, with just the edge turned back and stitched down to let the stripes show on the right side. The outer curtains, of much-faded rose silk, were re-made from a set of old bedroom curtains and these are interlined and lined so that they hang well and look properly opulent. The top pelmet or valance was pieced from various bits of old silk patchwork quilts, because I thought it would be a decorative way of using them up and because every room needs a bit of black—especially one as gentle in colouring as this—to give guts and contrast. I stapled the striped roof and curtains in place, adding a striped ruffle inside to hide the staples and finish it off. A thick piece of canvas goes on top of the bed, above the stripy roof to keep dust out, and I screwed four wooden knobs, from old curtain poles, to the corners to give a touch of swagger.

If you described this room, with its dark draped curtains, amber-coloured wallpaper, black lacquer furniture, it would sound heavy and sombre, whereas in fact—thanks largely to the glowing texture and colour of the draped sofa—it is warm and vivid, proof that colourists can break the rules with advantage, especially when backed up by a collection of old textiles in wonderful colours.

Opposite page: *Bedrooms, beds, can be the merest token arrangement of mattresses on the floor and looped up mosquito net drapery and yet look casually grand and romantic thanks to a few barbaric or beautiful things, like embroidered silk cushions, a copper samovar, and gilt crown canopy. Dazzling Attic sunshine outside helps.*

111

Collecting Your Wits

Most people who start haunting flea markets, junk shops, jumble sales, demolition yards and other venues for treasure hunting on the cheap will end up sooner or later acquiring a mass of *things*. Things they fell in love with, had a hunch could be valuable, couldn't resist because they were so cheap, thought they might find a use for—there is always a reason, but the net result is that you have to impose some order on this pile of goodies or it starts glumly accumulating dust, looking forlorn, and suggesting to the world that it has taken you over. There are various ways of fighting back, and—depending on your personality—these seem to fall into three categories: collections, arrangements and still lifes. All of these approaches inject surprise and interest into a home, visual treats as deliberate as the Japanese lady's flower arrangement and scroll. They are a personal, informal art form: at their most studied, worthy of a museum showcase; at their most careless they can be inspiration for a painter, a happy impromptu juxtaposition of bits and pieces which might never have met if you had not collected them and thought of putting them together.

THE HARMLESS PASSION

Collections are immediately recognizable, being like decimal points, the same thing multiplied according to the limits of your purse, space and time. Not quite the same thing, of course, but many versions of the same thing—egg cups, toast-racks, stamps, horse brasses, paste buckles, snuff boxes. Usually they are small, for convenience—it needs a Lord Montagu to collect vintage cars—and it helps if they are not already famously collectable, for the sake of affordability. Collectors are not quite like other people. Their mania for more, better, rarer examples is a passion rather than a hobby but, as passions go, harmless—and like the schoolboy's stamp collection, highly educational.

Whatever it is you collect, from enamel buttons to actors' memorabilia, you can't help learning all sorts of arcane, odd and useless facts along the way, and nothing so charges up a country weekend as the possibility of adding to your feather boa collection at the WI jumble sale, or your corn dolly collection at a craft bazaar or a Harvest Home. Collecting adds drama and excitement, the thrill of the chase, to the collector's life, and when the results are visually interesting and imaginatively presented, it can spread a little pleasure into other peoples' lives too. Presentation is a key word here, as provincial museums are fast discovering. A hundred white china toast-racks are ninety-

I think Michael B. White, shown here, must have had a lot of fun collecting all the idiosyncratic bits and pieces that make up a personal collage on his walls, and even more fun arranging them, just so, into a gentle parody of a trophy-hung hunting lodge. What have an assegai and a pelota basket in common? Probably nothing and it doesn't matter because even though some of the trophies are good, some joky, some quite pointless, they all in some mysterious way work together.

Above left: *Architectural student Joan Barnett hit on the idea of copying background detail in favourite paintings by Gauguin, Cezanne and Matisse as wall decoration. Colours, brushstrokes and spacing of a pattern like this posy are reproduced by hand.*

Above right: *Patchworks of Victorian tiles in sympathetic colours can hardly help making a wonderful wall. This one is in a kitchen. Jan Pienkowski, designer and illustrator, has a bathroom based on the same notion. Collecting enough tiles takes time but the chase adds zest to weekend trips to junk markets, country auction rooms. Note how the shelves here have been backed with a soft version, cloth patchwork, of the wall finish.*

Opposite page: *Absolute proof that an arrangement is more than the sum of its parts. The open fan, black as a Japanese headdress, a silk rose, an old picture hat nonchalantly taking a turn as lampshade—nothing here that almost any young girl could not assemble on her dressing-table, but how strangely evocative and* fin de siècle *the whole effect.*

nine too many for most households. Arranged with graphic wit on dark wooden shelves in a dull corner, they have a whole new lease of life, the calligraphic effect much more than the sum of its individual parts.

THE HAPPY GROUPING

Arrangements are not collections, because repetition is the last thing they aim for. Nor are they quite still lifes, being too self-conscious, too deliberately exquisite, to suit the painter who trusts his or her style to impose order and beauty, and doesn't want it ready made. Arrangements are the aesthete's silent homage to the intrinsic interest of things in themselves, which can be knowingly heightened and intensified by contrasting them with other, quite different, even discordant things. Arrangers—celebrated ones include David Hicks, Robin and Tricia Guild—enjoy playing with contrasts of style, texture, purpose, period, value; the richer and more capricious the mix and the greater the tension—the more achieved and memorable the arrangement.

Arrangements are not intended to last for ever; even moving the bits and pieces to dust them (and dusty arrangements are for the birds) can mar their inner harmony, but for a brief and privileged moment a sensitive arranger compels you to see, freshly, the ferocious power of a tribal mask, the sparkling frivolity and wit of an enamelled Easter egg, the luscious texture of a creamy lump of carved jade or the radical innocence of a sprig of apple blossom. Or it could be, a minute later, a boxwood shoe last, a chunk of amethyst quartz, an early radio and a carved crystal chess piece. A good arrangement is like an inspired menu, or a haiku poem, the distillation of a certain sort of pleasure in, and knowledge of, things or sensations. Arrangements require, being artificial and temporary, dramatic lighting and a suitably elegant stage: spotlights on glass-topped coffee tables seem to fit the bill quite well or, in another scenario, planks of smoke-coloured driftwood and the soft brilliance of an oil lamp.

Little Things Mean a Lot

There comes a moment in putting a place together, when one is suddenly over the hump. The time of big decisions, big expense, hard slog is past, the last carpenter and painter have packed up and left and one's place begins to feel like a home instead of a building site. Everyone needs a break at this point. One friend told me that doing up a house always left her with something like post-natal depression, drained of will-power and energy. After a while, though, as you feel your way into your new domain, experiencing it at different times and in different moods, you begin to notice things that didn't strike you at first, or didn't seem important when you were worrying about tiling the kitchen or which way round to position the bath. Critically, you wonder if the fresh pink paint in the bedroom isn't a little bland. All the door-handles, you suddenly observe, are tatty plastic. The window blinds are fine during the daytime but they don't give the room a cosy feeling at night. There seem to be a lot of bare walls suddenly, and bleakly empty corners.

This dissatisfied niggling is quite healthy. What it means is that you are working up to the second phase of decorating, which is the much more pleasurable, leisurely one of filling in the detail. This is when people are often visited by sudden inspirations, stencilling borders, hanging pictures a new way, shifting furniture around, filling a corner with plants. It is another way of taking possession of your territory, and making it unmistakably your own. The satisfaction it gives is out of all proportion to the outlay involved, in time or money. Money is what most people are short of at this stage, so the following list of ideas for rounding out or cheering up the new des. res. are mostly cheap and all ones you can tackle yourself. These inspirations can come from anywhere, but mostly from the sort of places women excel at creating—comfortable, pretty, vivid, cossetted. If you look around rooms like these, you will usually find this sort of attention to detail contributing to the warmly personal atmosphere.

DECORATIVE FLOURISHES

Decorative borders do a lot for a plainly painted room. If it lacks a cornice or the ceiling is oppressively high, a quite deep band round the ceiling can be stencilled to break up the wall surface colourfully and improve a room's proportions. If the existing wall colour is strong or dark, painting out the border area in a contrasting colour and stencilling on top, will make it stand out more. Use standard emulsion (pencil a guideline first) or acrylic gesso, which has greater coverage and dries fast. If the walls are painted a pale shade,

Pale blue and white can be chilly, or it can be calm, fresh and pretty as in this urban-cottagey-style drawing-room, where the limpid colour scheme holds the cheerful confusion of flowers, whatnots and knick-knacks together. Vivid yellow, as in the loose-covered chair, is wonderful with pale blue (such as Dulux Forget-me-not vinyl matt); as are polished floorboards, a patterned dhurrie, a parasol.

A Flourish with Wallpaper
John Dinkie, curator of the
Brighton Pavilion, arrived at
splendid walls by papering them
with large squares of marbled
paper then grouting (he says this
makes all the difference) between
these with Polyfilla. To protect the
paper and give it a sheen, it can
be varnished with thinned polyurethane, white shellac or emulsion
glaze. Be careful to experiment
first, though, as some papers take
varnish patchily.

simply stencil round in a darker or contrast colour, using the border to highlight any attractive features such as a sloping roof or nice alcoves. The simplest potato print technique using poster colour can look good—it may smudge here and there, but this hardly shows overall and has its own charm, sharpening and tightening up the architecture of all but the most beautiful rooms in a gratifying way, and it really doesn't take long. Also, fussing up a room like this makes it look more inhabited, and cared for—*soigné* as the French would say. In old houses trust your eye as much as a ruler or tape when finding the horizontal guideline, because usually everything is off-centre to some degree. Borders look stronger enclosed by straight painted lines. A thicker line in the same colour can be painted round doors, windows and above the skirting for more definition and a 'finished' look.

If you can't bear the thought of painting another inch, consider other possibilities which give a similar effect. Snip lacy cut-out borders in coloured paper, and just paste them down flat. There are plain paper bands, too, crisp in a contrast colour. Or use commercial printed borders. If all this seems too frilly and feminine, plain webbing or painted battens tacked in place look good.

There are many other decorative painting tricks to consider: patterning the flat fronts of built-in cupboards; picking out the mouldings on doors and shutters with a subtle contrast colour or silver leaf (aluminium transfer leaf, in fact, but no one can tell the difference); painting or stencilling a large motif as big as a picture above the fireplace if you are short on artwork (use American stencils, Hungarian embroidery, Aztec wall paintings, as inspiration); treating yourself to a sky ceiling, a currently fashionable conceit (cerulean blue paint with white clouds sponged on, faintly shadowed for drama with dirty yellowy-grey); painting out the interior of glazed cupboards or furniture in a rich brown-red, cerulean or apple green; painting your fireplace, if it is sombre wood, to match the walls, or marbled, sponged or flecked like porphyry. Porphyry is child's play to do, though it helps to look at a slab of the real thing first (visit the Sir John Soane museum). First you paint it the base colour, a deep brown-red, then over this you spatter white, then pink, then black. Surrounding walls and surfaces need masking off with newspaper. Spattering is done by taking the paint colour (one part undercoat, three parts white spirit, plus tinting colour) on a stiff brush and running your fingers sharply across it to release a shower of paint dots—practice on paper first. When dry, varnish well. Another trick which looks unexpectedly convincing and imposing, is to paint walls—preferably a cool stone colour—with white and sepia lines, to suggest ashlar courses (see pages 167–168).

QUILTING

Quilting to me means machine quilting, because I haven't time to sit stitching by hand on a frame, beautiful as that looks when completed. The wonder of quilting is that it makes the flimsiest fabric look rich, hang superbly and suggest warmth and luxury. Cheap calico, quilted, is good enough for curtains, whereas it would look flimsy made up the usual way. Decorators are soft on quilting and you will see quilted chintz chair covers, quilted satin cushion covers, quilted table skirts and bed coverlets. Odd scraps of beautiful old silk and velvet can be quilted to strengthen them and they then make superlative cushion covers. To machine quilt, the fabric needs to be loosely tacked to lining (calico or sheeting) and interlining, for which polyester padding, sold in various thicknesses at John Lewis, is practical if not as sensuous as lambswool or cotton batting, as used in the old days. Quilted curtains, run up and down or trellis stitched, look sumptuous, of course, but these take a long time. (Incidentally, ready-quilted cotton prints are available at many big department stores.) But just a small area of quilting in a room gives it a luxurious feeling. Try quilting the material to cover a chair seat or a few cushions. On shiny fabric, like satin, it gives great richness of texture. Finish all quilting off with a neat coloured border, like an old bed quilt would have. Always use good quality polyester thread to machine quilt—cheaper threads just keep snapping. And don't force the machine too much—when it seems to be overheating, switch off and let it cool down.

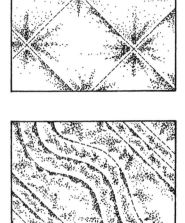

Three styles of hand-stitched traditional quilting (above). Loose tacking stitches sandwich polyester padding between a calico backing and top fabric (below).

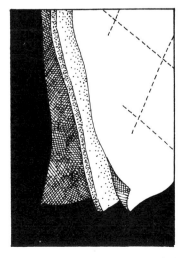

PICTURE HANGING

A fine painting, well framed, can make a room come to life like nothing else. However, there is no reason to leave walls blank because one cannot afford a Dufy or a Matisse, a set of Piranesi engravings or an original Hockney. There are many sources of cheaper artwork for wall decoration. Old photographs, maps, prints or coloured plates (there is, for instance, a stall in London's Farringdon Road with boxes full of plates ripped out of old books and this is echoed on other stalls throughout the country), one's own or one's children's paintings and sketches—almost anything interesting or decorative can be immensely enhanced by making a fuss of it, mounting, framing and hanging it attractively. A whole wall packed with artwork of every sort, is even more lively and stimulating than a whole wall packed with books. It doesn't have to be great art, necessarily, but personal and quirkish like a large doodle pad. Why not buy up junk frames in jumble sales and flea markets, paint them

bright colours and fit them round children's pictures. I have begun a modest collection of sepia photographs, mostly in oak or maple frames with cream mounts, with which I hope to plaster my study walls in due course. Some people have a thing about old cartoons or pin-up photos of yesteryear. The rule is if it is worth looking at, frame it, because all but the most distinguished work—which needs nothing, though it never suffers from being superlatively framed—is tripled in strength and interest by intelligent mounting and framing.

Hanging is the next problem. One small picture on a large blank wall looks nothing. One large picture or several smaller ones grouped, makes a different impact, especially if they are anchored by seating or some other piece of furniture below. A series of prints always gains from mounting and framing identically, even if they are of different sizes. Disparate groups of old prints, oval framed, or black and gilt Hogarthian frames can be drawn together visually by Nancy Lancaster's trick of looping a cord, tasselled both ends, from an apex, and down and out over the pictures like a tent. A grander series, matching perhaps, can be linked decoratively by a wide ribbon, ending in a clover-leaf bow at the top. Watered silk or moiré is the proper ribbon to use though this does, of course, only suit a certain type of room, furnished with antiques, elegant if not grand. I love old silhouettes and often wonder why no one has revived this sprightly form of portraiture. It is only a matter of arranging the sitter and the lighting to cast a shadow one can pencil round. Filled in with Indian ink, mounted and framed in gilt, these make characterful wall decoration, with a real family interest.

Children love sticking up things on their walls. If you mind the way this pockmarks walls, make them pinboards to encourage them to concentrate their attentions. Both felt and hessian come in a wonderful range of colours and can be glued or stapled over a square of chipboard. I jazzed up some of my own pinboards, which looked too foursquare and office-like, by sticking some left-over Indian print around the edges to frame them. What is fun about pinboards, of course, is that they are one's own changing exhibition—scraps cut from colour supplements, offers you plan to send off for, postcards, taxi cab numbers, all the odds and ends you enjoy looking at or forget if you tidy them away.

MIRRORS

I never feel any room is complete without at least one mirror. Mirrors give a room sparkle, mystery. They can be used to reflect light back by hanging them opposite a window, but I almost prefer them hung sideways to the light source or on the window wall itself, where they create a pleasing ambiguity, as if you had an extra window dematerializing the solid masonry. If, like me, you prefer old, grey mirror glass with dark spots where the silvering has worn off or with yellow fly stains, building up a collection is not difficult, unless you also insist on eighteenth-century gilt frames. Old dressing-table mirrors or mirrored cupboard doors can be converted into wall mirrors by unscrewing the handles or swivel pins, filling the holes and screwing mirror plates to the back. Strip off crude varnish for a plain wood finish or paint them. Look for bevelled mirrors—this small extra adds sparkle and visual interest. The glass will be thicker, too. I stencilled a white border round a mirror for fun, and while it means taking extra care cleaning the surface, the lacy effect improved a very plain glass and frame.

Hang mirrors, if you can, so that they reflect lights back into the room. When houses were lit by candles, mirrors played an important part in intensifying the light in a room. This brought about a vogue for mirrored candle sconces or pier glasses and overmantel mirrors with candleholders either side of the frame. Electric light is less romantic but, even so, the effect of warmly shaded lights reflected back and forth is always alluring.

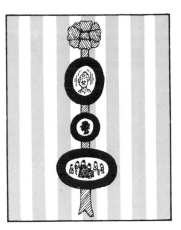

An elegant and effective way of grouping small pictures is to hang them on a wide silk ribbon knotted at the top in a clover leaf.

A junk mirror made from a picture frame creates a breathing space on a busy wall (transfer gold leaf, stencils, glazed paint finishes) in this astonishing room. Dining chairs are standard garden wicker upgraded with shiny black spray paint.

121

Covering whole walls with mirror is an old decorator's trick for dissolving a room's contours and opening up walls. Now that sheets of mirror-surfaced plastic are available quite cheaply, this is an effect anyone can try. Smoked, antiqued or otherwise subtilized mirror finishes look best—a huge expanse of dazzlingly bright mirror lacks mystery and makes people feel uneasy. French decorators are fond of sheeting the chimney-breast wall with smoky mirror, cut to fit around the fireplace. Then—and this *jeu d'esprit* always takes the eye—they like to hang a framed mirror on top. Mirroring alcoves each side of the fireplace, sofa or whatever, is another ruse to think about. Using shadowy tinted mirror, this opens up a room and makes a grandly reflective back-drop to lamps, flowers or, best of all, a collection of coloured glass, which can be arranged on glass shelves so they seem to float in mid-air. The same idea can be used to back a cabinet or wall cupboard. Wherever possible, try to integrate large expanses of mirror into a room's architecture. If it isn't going wall to wall but covering one section of a wall, framing it with a moulding painted to match the walls will give it a handsome air of solidity.

A decorating firm which shall be nameless had the idea of covering one wall of a typically dark, narrow London front hall with mirror tiles. The effect could not have been more misjudged. Firstly, the tiles were shiny bright, next they ended arbitrarily just before the first bend in the wall without a moulding to anchor them visually and, lastly, they were hung on the wrong wall—the one behind the door instead of the one opposite, which would have reflected back light. Instead of making the hall look light and glamorous, it looked tacky and vaguely lavatorial and the temptation was to rush by head down to escape a brutally revealing reflection. Anyone thinking of trying that sort of illusionism needs to be a bit clever. If both walls were sheeted—not tiled—in a dusky mirror glass and then some attractive murals were painted on to the glass, so that one seemed to look between pillars or trellised arches, there would be a real sense of opening up limitless spaces, marvellous at night if wall sconces or lights reflected back from each side. In general, though, theatrical gestures like this are best avoided unless one is going to carry them off with style and conviction. A mirrored wall behind the bath, on the other hand, does wonders for a small bathroom if you like seeing yourself close to. Practical too, even if they do steam up. Another surprising but attractive use of mirror I remember, was behind a canopied bed pushed up against a wall. Because the canopy and bed curtains made a little tent of the bed, so that the mirror was only glimpsed mysteriously from the room, there was an inviting suggestion of mysterious space.

Designers and decorators have always enjoyed playing with the deceiving and reflective properties of mirror glass. In rococo houses they were used on ceilings, to fill fireplaces in summer, and to back shutters which slid into the panelling by day and at night were closed to echo the mirrors used on walls opposite. Variants on this theme have been used by modern decorators with great success. Mirrors on the backs of folding shutters, for instance, are much more appealing to my eye than the great mirrored doors currently favoured on built-in bedroom cupboards. Sir John Soane used small mirrored insets in the front of his shutters, so that window light sparkled off them beguilingly—an easy idea to copy (remove the mouldings, have glass cut to fit the inner panel, replace the mouldings) and one that enlivens a room.

I like mirror used in playful, unexpected ways. Mirror mosaic, which comes in sheets with a flexible backing which can be cut with scissors and then glued down, is great fun to play with. I lined a plastered window reveal in my kitchen with it, out of curiosity. Afterwards I grouted all the cracks and joins with grouting compound stained red with powder colour to match the walls. It looked festive, a little Indian. What I would really have liked to do—but thought of too late—was bed tiny mirrors into the wall plaster before

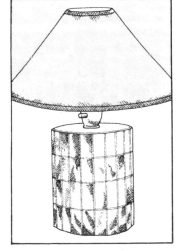

Mirror mosaic can turn the most unspectacular household furnishings into glittering curios.

painting a lavish Indian-type design on top. That would look ravishing, if one had the patience, like Gujarati embroideries with their little mirror discs twinkling out of the vivid flowers. Indian palace walls often do explore the magic of tiny mirrored points, set into a flat mural pattern—at night these sparkle out like stars. Rumour has it that the mirrors replace precious stones, filched over the years, but I think I would be just as happy with mirrors. It would be a brave soul who tried to talk a typical British plasterer into such freakish experiments, however. On the other hand, they might co-operate to the extent of letting you set strips of mirror mosaic into the walls, outlining a fireplace maybe, or making a dazzling line just below the cornice.

Where a small window looks out on sooty walls, replacing clear glass with mirror glass makes an eyesore into a feature. In bathrooms or lavatories this could be done over part of the window only, concealing the inmates from prying eyes, without blocking off all the natural light.

WINDOW TREATMENTS

In most cases, windows without curtains look too bare, like eyes without lashes. Old houses have deep reveals or shutter boxes, which soften incoming light. These can dispense with curtains, except for warmth or cosiness. Houses or rooms without these need curtains or blinds to mediate between outside light and the light within the room.

Lots of glass equals lots of class. Old gilt framed mirrors of different shapes and sizes are as refreshing to the eye as water in this tenderly coloured, very pretty, very feminine sitting-room. Note how the magnificent blue of the ceramic pot stand lifts the room's other gentle pastels and soft crimson red.

People often object to curtains for blocking out light, not realizing that many rooms look all the better for having some of the light softened or filtered through fabric. Traditional windows invariably had some form of treatment, its elaboration increasing with the size of the window, from skinny padded curtains in Jacobean times, through the festoon type popular in the eighteenth century, to the looped-back curtains with swagged and draped pelmets which were used on the much bigger windows of the nineteenth century. For a pair of tall windows in Regency times, it would have been quite usual to have two pairs of curtains, the outer ones of heavy material looped back, the inner pair diaphanous muslin. One curtain pole might run across the top of both windows and this would have supported a swagged, furled and draped pelmet in the classical revival style. What people then knew is that softening the light that comes in at the top of a window makes all the difference to the atmosphere of a room: quality of light rather than quantity was the aim. Pelmets and blinds both help to soften this top light and make a room and everything in it immediately more attractive. You can easily check the truth of this by tacking a piece of fabric over the top eighteen inches or so of your windows—if the room suddenly seems twice as inviting, your windows need something up top. Roller blinds and festoon blinds are the cheapest solution, though roller blinds look better with curtains in addition.

A pair of top-class curtains from a decorating firm, lined and interlined, can easily cost £1,000 these days. Curtains like these take a long time to make, but the sewing involved is straightforward and home-made ones cost a fraction of the price. There are several detailed instruction manuals on soft furnishings which tell you how to make them and also how to make blinds. A simpler type of curtain arrangement, which cuts out a lot of stitching, is to dispense with rings and run the curtain pole straight through a channel stitched in the curtain heading. Curtains like these cannot be drawn, they are looped back each side during the daytime (much like the curtains children draw) and this in itself acts as a light filter up top. I have seen a pair in cheap cotton canvas (which comes in many lengths and huge widths) threaded on to a wooden pole—and they look excellent.

The good thing about heavy traditional curtains, aside from the stately way they frame a window, is their warmth. Not till you have drawn a vast pair of velvet curtains across for the night do you realize how many whistling draughts a window admits. But there are cheaper ways of keeping warm. Ready quilted fabrics, like the sort sold for dressing gowns, can make good curtains, too, with built-in insulation. Quilted fabrics hang beautifully. From a wholesaler, fabrics like these work out absurdly cheap if you are lucky enough to find a design and colour you like—a couple of pounds a metre perhaps. Making up could not be simpler, just bind the edges with a contrasting fabric and stitch rufflette tape across the top.

If warmth is not your problem and you hate sewing, a certain airy classical effect can be achieved by fixing up a pole and simply folding a length of sheeting round it, tacked up here, stapled there, till you like the look. It is a 'pure' look, best interpreted in plain white or natural coloured cottons—lawn, sheeting by the yard, finest grade canvas. The French do this sort of thing expertly, so casually that the fabric seems to be lightly blown into position. In their knowing way, however, they usually offset this unstudied simplicity in one sector of the room with elegance in another, perhaps an exquisite needleworked antique sofa standing in front. It is a sophisticated game, this playing off of the elaborate and the simple, the very costly and the very cheap—the costly things lend authority to the cheap (so one would never suppose the sheeted windows were a stop-gap while the real curtains were at the cleaners, for instance) and the cheap things lessen the bourgeois pretensions of the costly ones. Ornamentalist designers tend to leave out the needle-

'Valerie had some very lovely curtains at the windows of the long salotto looking on the river, curtains of queer, ancient material that looked like finely knitted silk, most beautifully faded down from vermilion and orange and gold and black to a sheer soft glow. Valerie hardly ever came into the salotto without mentally falling on her knees before the curtains.

"Chartres," she said, "to me they are Chartres."'

'Things' D. H. LAWRENCE

124

worked sofa element, the good piece that anchors the rest, and the result is a room where everything looks provisional, temporary. It can have a freakish chic, but it lacks what the French call '*serieux*'.

A prettier interpretation of the under-dressed window is with lace panels. Some clever people have been collecting and hoarding antique lace panels for years—they could be bought cheaply in flea markets then. Lace is in full revival now and the new copies of the old machine-made panels cost more than the old ones used to. Never mind, they are still cheaper than regular curtains, and hoicked up over a window their filigree delicacy is as flattering as a bridal veil. They give more privacy than one would suppose but, if you use them in a bedroom, this might be something you want to check.

GEWGAWS AND TRIFLES

Dressing a room or a room-set for photography is fascinating proof of the integrity of a real, lived-in place which has evolved, as against the blankness of the make-believe room one puts together hurriedly for a purpose. Given time, and a flexible brief, a good stylist can come up with an interior which is pretty or chic, imaginative or visually convincing. It looks like a real room, at first glance, if it incorporates old bits and pieces. It may even suggest atmosphere. But if you compare it with a photograph of a similar, but *real*, room the difference jumps out at you. The phoney room probably has much better things, more luxurious fabrics and upholstery, but surface glamour does not make up for lack of authenticity. It is simply impossible to raid furniture stores and antique shops and put together something which conveys the intimate relatedness of a place which has been assembled gradually. Rooms

Pretty bits and pieces like this desk set and mirror on a table is a great help in dressing up a room, an excuse for another lamp, some nice contrasty colours in the paper. Marbled paper makes the best lampshades, different looking, but flattering.

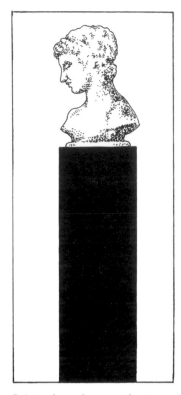

Paint a cheap plaster cast bust in a stone colour, rub on shoe polish to simulate age and feature it.

with style—real rooms—are charged with the personality of their occupants. They are stamped with all the choices of colours, furniture, fabrics and patterns but, most of all or most powerfully, in the inessentials—all those objects a person adds to the basic scheme for their beauty or charm or associations. It is that inner tale which no 'accessorizing scheme', as one breezy Californian designer phrased it, can begin to suggest. It is an observable fact that style cannot be delegated—rooms can be assembled by decorators and filled with rare, beautiful things, but without some personal involvement by their owners they do not come alive.

What you add to a room in the way of pictures, knick-knacks, lamps, ashtrays, books and pots is not a top-dressing of accessories, but a layer of visible autobiography. This gives them a value and interest quite separate from their intrinsic rarity or cost. Personally, I like to see things out in the open, not frozen in display cabinets, grouped perhaps to make a visual point—a cluster of old brown stoneware jugs displaying their opalescent sheen, a small forest of spiky iron candlesticks—but not too self-consciously 'an arrangement'. Found things, *objets trouvés*, have an honourable place in this personal exhibition—pebbles and shells picked up on holidays, driftwood hollowed and bleached like outlandish bones and, best of all, the discarded object for which one has found a new use. I remember vividly the small anchor which T. E. Lawrence had his local blacksmith convert into a door knocker at his cottage in Bovington. But most personal and poetically evocative of all are those clusters of things, both functional and decorative, disposed on top of a desk or dressing-table, sometimes by a stove or on a kitchen windowsill, which have arrived at an almost ritual interrelationship over the years. These, like the fireplace with its special little frieze of mementoes, are the altars of the household gods. Modest, but meaningful, they take one straight to the heart of a place—in a way no Fabergé Easter egg or collection of Netsuke ivory could ever match. Untouched, unvisited things become forlorn, however beautiful.

A SOFTENING INFLUENCE

Rooms with a look of softness about them are extraordinarily inviting. The softness I am thinking of is not so much the plumpness of cushions puffy with down (though snatch these up when you find them) or of feminine frills and falderals, as the kindly sensuousness of varied textures—plush, crisp, mellow, brilliant—the delicate tactile contrasts which the masters of still life painting explore so voluptuously. Old textiles are among the most evocative of collectables when it comes to setting mood and creating atmosphere. It is still possible to find and afford strange and beautiful fragments of old needlework, *petit point*, old hand-knotted lace, hand-woven fabrics. Less ambitiously, printed chenille table covers—I have one, a pound or two from the local market, ink stained and cigarette burnt, but so rosily glowing it warms a whole corner—machine-made lace a little yellowed, crocheted pillowcases, velvet curtains their colours exhausted by time: these can all discharge something of an aura wherever they come to roost. There are innumerable uses for these waifs and strays, however fragmentary. Patterned lengths, whole enough or substantial enough in design, can be used to soften and decorate a blank wall. I missed the only chance I ever had of acquiring a 'verdure' tapestry, one of those ravishing, discoloured pastoral scenes, all blues, greens and sandy buffs (if you look on the back you find the postcard colours of the original), but I have a square of woven damask in the same colours which will go on a wall when I have found a way to conceal its disgraceful rents. Fabrics on walls give warmth and texture quite undemandingly. Where paintings claim your attention, they quietly recede.

Old fabrics can be draped over sofas and chairs, one at a time, or in

'Molly went up to her little bedroom, clean and neat as a bedroom could be, with draperies of small delicate patchwork—bed-curtains, window curtains and counterpane; a japanned toilet table, full of little boxes, with a small looking-glass affixed to it, that distorted every face that was so unwise as to look in it. This room had been to the child one of the most dainty and luxurious places ever seen, in comparison with her own bare, white-dimity bedroom; and now she was sleeping in it as a guest and all the quaint adornments she had once peeped at as a great favour . . . were set out for her use.'

'Wives and Daughters'
ELIZABETH GASKELL

Another vivid corner of a dealer's house, with its amber-toned walls flecked to look like bird's eye maple, and lots of vivid pink for contrast on the floor, cushion, embroidered cloth. The Victorian painted chair with its scrap decoration is a real dealer's piece.

layers if you like that impromptu *deshabillé* effect. Some look rich and romantic dripping over tables, round or rectangular. Some feminine rooms have swooningly pretty tables skirted in layers of lace-edged linen, but this takes living up to and much laundering. Sober, but very grand, is the oblong table covered—Renaissance style—with a fine rug; a plushy, fringed chenille cloth has the same effect, though that takes us up to Victoriana. Squashy-looking things, which could be pouffes or stools as well as cushions, gain great prestige from being covered in scraps of kelim, too tattered to lay on the floor. And not just kelim—anything in the carpet line with solid texture and softened colour makes a place look more kindly.

Odd, beautiful, interesting scraps seem destined to cover cushions. They can be pieced, used straight if they are large enough, or eked out by bits of suitably worn velvet or ribbon. Making a pretty, charming thing from odds and ends is oddly satisfying. But don't throw all that labour away by using it to cover a lumpy bag of kapok or a perky cube of foam. Pure down, or down and feathers, is the only filling possible for a special cushion.

Small refinements can add to the finish of a room, curtain tiebacks, for instance, made of three sausages of fabric plaited together. Lampshades in peach-coloured silk are lovely and vast slips turn up in markets, cut on the bias, ideal for covering shades. And, while you are about it, don't overlook what the trade calls 'trimmings', fringes, tassels, cords, gimp, braid. The old ones were intricately made, from fibres like silk, gold thread or wool and a few lengths stitched round a cushion or lampshade add considerable class.

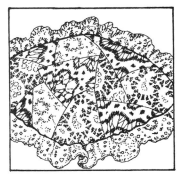

Scraps of old lace pieced over a coloured silk backing makes the prettiest cushions.

Lighting Up

Everyone agrees that successful lighting is one of the most difficult things for amateurs to get right. It should be flattering to the place and the people but practical, too, so that work areas, landings and front doors, are adequately lit. It is important to get it right because fittings and installation are expensive and yet, however carefully one plans, in practice, something invariably turns out to be in the wrong place—lamp sockets are inaccessible behind large heavy pieces of furniture; the balance of light in a room is uneasy, too glaring in one part, too dark in another. If I could afford it, the one thing I would pay someone else to plan out for me would be a sophisticated lighting arrangement, which would give exactly the type of lighting I had in mind for each room. It is not simply the placing of lights which is difficult—actually that is the easiest part—but making sure that the overall effect is fairly even, without being harsh, at the right level in relation to one's eyes when standing and sitting, and that things which need illumination, like bookcases or beautiful objects or pictures, are not lost in the shadows. It may cheer you to know that almost everyone whose rooms were photographed for this book was envious of the intense but diffused light created by photographic reflectors—most of those radiant interiors one sees in magazines are photographers' magic, rather than super-subtle lighting schemes.

The system to choose depends on whether a room decor or furnishing is static or may be changed around often and, of course, on what you have to spend. The non-expert solution, which is cheaper, more flexible and lets you experiment before committing yourself to lengthy, messy installation work, is the traditional one of table lamps dotted about the room, linked to a dimmer switch to adjust the intensity. The latter is an optional extra, but it does give leeway, allowing overall lighting to be subdued at will without plunging whole areas into darkness, which is what happens when you simply switch one or two lamps off. Always, by the way, have torpedo switches on the flex, or switches on the light socket—scrabbling about on hands and knees looking for wall switches is exasperating. Table lamps are sited, as a rule, where they are most useful—on a desk, or table either side of a sofa. It is worth investing in good shades or learning to make your own. The best, in my experience, are of silk or fine fabric, covered in on top and lined, because this diffuses the light in the softest, warmest fashion. Shade carriers should be the right size, so that the light source—the naked bulb—is invisible, even when sitting down. Opalescent bulbs cut down glare, too, which is useful if your shades are thin.

Original and decidedly glam use of concealed lighting to create a flowery extra dimension to a small upstairs bedroom. Sash windows were replaced with long glazed doors opening on to a tiny balcony, too small to be taken seriously except as a sort of expanded windowsill to stand greenery on. One strong spotlight is all that is needed to silhouette leaves and flowers and make a dramatic contrast with the warm shaded light by the bed. Paint suggestion: Dulux Magnolia vinyl matt.

Room Lighting
Domestic lighting falls into three categories: directional (spots, downlighters); diffused (shaded lamps, concealed strip lighting); and decorative. 100 watt bulbs are recommended for any close work, like reading or sewing, and should preferably be in a directional lamp. Wall-mounted spotlights are good for reading in bed without keeping your partner awake.

The art of sophisticated lighting is to exploit the warmth and drama of light, without revealing the light source or allowing stray glare to unnerve the room's occupants. Table lamps, at a low level, bulbs hidden, create a low-level intimacy which immediately invites one to sit down and feel at ease. Drama can be introduced, flexibly, by uplighters, which can be hidden behind chairs, curtains, anywhere, so that they cast an upward glow which brings anything special—pictures, books, a fine architectural feature—to one's attention. Underlit central areas can have a standard lamp sited close by (floor sockets are the chic thing here, avoiding trailing flex) for use when needed for reading. Telly watching needs a light behind the viewers for balance and less eye strain. If you are going to have a sofa pushed back against the wall, wall-lights each side (the best are the brass-armed extending ones with shades) will cast a soft local light without demanding table lamps and more flexes. Large desks can take a desk lamp, smaller ones are better lit by a wall-mounted lamp to free surface space. Bedside lamps should be low to flatter and make reading comfortable, but near enough to switch off without an argument. Ideally, all bedroom lights should be switched off from the bed, a fact often overlooked.

While we are pursuing the simpler systems, the kitchen must be given its due attention. Architects and designers usually plump for the strip lights under wall cupboard system, for lighting work areas, cooker and sink as well as worktops. However, they insist that balance in a kitchen lighting arrangement is important—a bright ring of light round the circumference with darker areas where one eats is tiring to the eyes and spirits. More lighting over the eating area is needed, which can be a central light on an adjustable flex or recessed ceiling spots. Strip lights over the worktops should be tinted fluorescent, not tungsten—more expensive but no improvement—and, if the worktop and the backing are a warm natural material, like wood or clay tiles, the warmer light will be reflected back into the room, not the glare. Strip lights will, of course, be hidden behind a pelmet below wall cabinets or have a baffle shade. Downlighters should never be fixed into the ceiling above wall cabinets, because they are blocked by the cupboards and cast inconvenient shadows. Track lighting—silvered bulbs in silver reflectors give maximum

Creamy walls (Dulux Prelude vinyl silk, for instance) and cupboards, creamy ornamentalist caprices like the cheetah masks and Corinthian columns, creamy lighting, some of it running beneath the wall cupboards, some bouncing off the shiny ceiling, also cream. Note newly fashionable Thirties chair, more boat- than tub-shaped.

diffusion—works best when the light is bounced off walls. Beware: you will need more than you think. A dimmer switch is a handy cop-out with kitchen lighting and the extra expense is justified by the fact that dimmers save on bulbs. The cost in keeping a fancy ceiling track fitted out with special bulbs is something one learns later, to one's cost!

Bathroom lighting is governed by safety regulations and must be switched off by pull strings, rather than switches. Shaving and applying make-up are the bathroom activities that demand specific, local light, honestly revealing without being so harsh and cold one backs off in dismay. Wall-lights each side of the mirror are probably the best solution—I find those star's dressing-room lighting arrangements, with bulbs on a track round the mirror, glamorous.

Overhead lighting, diffused by kindly shades, is probably the simplest efficient solution for landings, corridors and hallways, though wall-lights, if you have the fittings already, give a more attractive light, and are needed on long flights of stairs, with half-landings. Keep these neat and tight to the wall, at about eye-level. Wall-mounted spots are good in passages, where you are on the move, especially when focused on something eye-catching on the wall opposite, but they are disconcerting in rooms where one sits, because somewhere or other the naked bulb glares out at someone.

The cost of installing or re-wiring even these quite simple lighting systems, especially if you add dimmers, is enough. So, ultra-sophisticated systems are probably only for the people rich enough to call in a designer and pay for all the ripping up of floorboards or down of ceilings, and the subsequent re-decoration. But for anyone whose ceilings are already down, or floors up, it may be worth thinking about some more recherché solutions. That glamorous, starry, soft but brilliant lighting Americans are so good at, usually relies on recessed ceiling spots, but not just a few, more likely one every yard or so above seating areas, desks, drinks table. Then add to that the crafty pencil spots focused on pictures, statues, other goodies. If the recessed lights are doing their stuff properly, which means they are more expensive both to buy and install, they are set so high up in the ceiling that you enter this light-bathed atmosphere without ever being aware of the light source.

Hall Lighting
High, narrow front halls could benefit visually by dropping the ceiling level using a grid (of translucent panels in a timber frame) suspended below overhead lighting, in the form of fluorescent tubes or spots.

Pendant hall or landing lights cast a softer, more flattering glow in bowl or lantern-type shades, which conceal the glaring bulbs. Try glass or alabaster bowls on chains (from junk shops) for this effect.

131

Top Floors

Taking up floors in a house at ground level, because of dry rot or to put in a damp-proof course, is an excellent opportunity to consider putting down something more exciting, nearer to a *matière noble* than common deal planks. The weight of the nobler materials—stone, marble and so on—makes them very expensive to install above ground level, since joists will need reinforcing and a stout timber base is still needed to lay flags, marble or tiles over. However, where the original floor was laid over earth or concrete, these problems do not arise. After the damp-proof membrane has been installed and concreted in, you are free to play around with all sorts of possibilities, not all of them outrageously expensive, if you are clever, lucky or a bit of both.

Artist David Versey laid a bathroom floor of Roman opulence in his house, using stacks of abandoned marble washstand tops (see page 85). That was luck, if you like. The clever part was finding a way of cutting them to size himself with a power tool using a metal-cutting attachment, which had to be replaced often, but still brought the cost in well under the figure a marble-cutting firm (monumental masons would be the people to speak to here) would have charged, not to mention the bother of transporting them to and fro. Artists seem to have a feel for imaginative floorings. Polly Hope covered some of the floors of her Greek island home with black and white pebbles arranged in patterns, or plain grey pebbles (see page 140). To make a pebbled floor surface, sections are boarded off with plank frames, concrete poured in to a depth of approximately 2 inches (5 cm)—about two-thirds the length of the pebbles—and the pebbles set in either by hand or shovelled on and raked flat with a long-handled implement like a toothless rake. After the concrete has hardened sufficiently to walk on, you go over the surface with a stiff brush, to smooth it off between the pebbles, and tidy it up. As one section is completed, the frames are taken up and moved on to the adjacent space. A plain cobbled floor would be tough and attractive in a holiday cottage or a garden room. On terraces or courtyards, cobbles are often used with bricks or stone or concrete paving slabs, to give a variegated surface, both handsome and highly durable. Cobbles help to humanize the slightly too regular effect of concrete slabs, as do bricks and granite setts.

Concrete paviours can be humanized, as Diana Phipps found when she had them laid, as a down-market version of York stone, in her converted barn (see page 32). Laid smooth side up, grouted with cement coloured to match, then varnished, rubbed with a little oil colour—greyish, brownish, yellowish—and a final couple of varnishes, they make an amazingly convincing stone-flagged floor. To improve the colour she rubs in a little shoe polish—light tan,

Stone paving, worn by time, unsoftened by rugs or colour of any kind, makes a severely handsome floor to this studio-sitting room in the country. With all the emphasis on shape and line, it's the rustic version of the urban designer look shown on pages 18–19.

The tough good looks of russet brown floor tiles, arranged in a herringbone weave, is a counterpoint to the splendid patchwork table and divan base built by David Versey from end-grain wood blocks rescued from roadworks—in some places they were used to surface roads. David had to sand away layers of pitch before glueing and cramping the blocks together—a great something-for-nothing coup.

perhaps or black—from time to time.

Brick floors are good in kitchens, utility rooms, garden rooms, anywhere you need a hard durable floor with a pleasant, variegated texture and colour. If suitable bricks can be found second hand, the savings will be considerable and you have the bonus of weathered colour. Make sure the baked surface is still intact though—bricks gone friable will gradually powder away. Check, too, that not too much cleaning off of old mortar is needed, because this doubles the time the job takes. I have brick floors in kitchen and back hall, laid on their sides, four one way, four the opposite, like brick stitch in tapestry. An occasional coat of varnish—I use yacht varnish, for strength— unifies the texture, brings up the colours and keeps the dust down.

Stone flags, if you are lucky enough to find them *in situ*, should be treasured. Clean them, bleach them, seal and wax them, to bring them to a dull shine. If you can, though, leave them where they are, a little uneven, worn down by passing feet. Unless you number the stones, re-laying could land you in unforeseen trouble and making them pancake flat tends to rob them of much of their beauty. Old tiles or mosaics should equally be respected, as they are not only strong and good looking, but increasingly valuable features in any old house. Mosaics often have missing bits which can be restored, either by you from standard mosaic pieces or by professionals working in this medium. At a pinch, fill in missing pieces with grouting compound, coloured to match—if you leave gaps the surrounding pieces are liable to shift and fall out too.

Second-hand quarry tiles can be found in architectural salvage centres, rather cheaper than new, thicker in section and more kindly in colour. These look best laid close and even. Large *provençal*-type tiles, with agreeably uneven surfaces, as well as many other handmade-looking tiles, look handsomer for being set some distance apart —nearer $\frac{1}{2}$ inch (1 cm) than the conventional $\frac{1}{16}$ inch (1 or 2 mm) used on thin modern tiles —and grouted in off-white. For some reason this emphasizes their picturesqueness.

The cheapest possible floor of this sort is made of fine-textured sand and cement, stained a good colour like black or dark red, and then gone over with a steel float to polish it to a fine, even texture like plaster. Floors like this can be rounded off where they meet the walls, making a smooth coving which is elegant and easy to keep clean. French plasterers and masons excel at this sort of up-market yet heavy-duty floor, and I live in hope that their British counterparts may follow suit.

What is so heartening about all the floors I have been discussing is that their solidity makes the whole building feel more solid. But wood floors have other beauties, like warmth, texture and resilience.

Wide, old oak planks, dark and shiny, are best left alone though they can do with frequent rubbing up—an electric polisher is a wonderfully efficient gadget. Any badly beaten-up plank floor, deal plus varnish stain or paint or both, is most rapidly cleaned and levelled by sanding long and hard, after first punching down nails and lifting tacks. Think first before levelling older floors—these have wider, thicker boards—because the wear and tear of time has probably given them an appealing texture, a little ridged or hollowed. It is astonishing how splendid they can look when cleaned off by hand, stained, varnished and waxed. Sanding off the surface would rob them of much of their character. On the other hand, cleaning them is usually a painstaking, arduous task, best done with a scraper and/or paint stripper where necessary. Cabinetmakers' suppliers will tell you what to use for staining them—the stains you mix yourself are a great deal cheaper than the proprietary ones sold in little tins. After staining, they need lightly sanding over, then thorough cleaning up before varnish is applied. Two or three coats of yacht varnish make the toughest possible finish, very shiny, but this will become rapidly subdued by use. Sand between coats for the best finish, really silky. Floor sealers are easier to apply and dry more quickly. They do not build up such a durable finish, though repeated waxing helps.

Deal floors which have been heavily sanded are yellowish and irritatingly knotty, all of which varnish or seal emphasizes. A better finish, if you want a pale floor, is had by rubbing greyish-white paint into the wood to leave a pale bloom over the surface, a bit driftwoody. It can then be varnished, to protect it. Alternatively, simply scour the planks with wet sand as they did in the eighteenth century to give a pretty, matt, bleached effect. Failing sand, use Vim. Be warned, though, this is hard work and only for people with overflowing energies. It might be simpler to stain your entire floor, either a currently fashionable black or one of the ravishing shades available in the new Dulux range of varnishes. These stain and varnish in one go and can be overlaid for extra rich colour tone: green over blue and so on. A rug somewhere warms them up.

Desperate plank floors are a case for paint. Sand, prime, undercoat and paint as for woodwork, but then varnish copiously, at least three coats. This will give a smooth, natty surface, very durable too. Its plainness invites decoration, and stencilled floors are pretty and popular. On a pale painted floor, soft flowery borders and motifs are charming, waking up the whole room. On darker colours, geometric-type repeating designs, modelled on tiles, look rich. Or you can go the whole way with the paint finishes and mark the floor out into squares, marbled with paint to suggest country house hall, Italian *loggias*, what you will.

Cleaning Floors
A 'stain-removing wash' marketed by W. S. Jenkins and Co. of Tottenham, London, will bleach out old engrained stain from wood floors without altering the colour of the wood. Any varnish should be removed first, with cellulose stripper, then the wash applied according to instructions. Local stains can be bleached out with a saturated solution of oxalic acid in water or meths—slop on then leave to dry before washing off. Most chemists sell oxalic crystals— explain what you want it for.

Use an orbital power sander to smooth varnish coats, moving from medium to fine grade sandpaper and travelling with the grain of the wood.

Indoor/Outdoor Rooms

The area where house and garden merge or interchange can be the chief delight of a place. It is hard to say which is more enjoyable, taking indoor comforts like food, drink and comfortable chairs outside, or taking outdoor pleasures, like scented flowers, green leaves and the fresh smell of growing plants, inside, into what the Edwardians called a conservatory but is now more likely to be a 'garden room'. Garden rooms are less dedicated to horticultural display than conservatories used to be. They tend to be tacked on to the most sheltered sunny wall of a house, to borrow warmth from the house as well as the sun, they are not so extensively glazed and they are likely to have easy chairs, floor coverings and shaded lights as well as a profusion of growing things, wooden shelving for plants, tubs of lilies or fuchsias, with probably a few sturdy creepers looping across the glazing bars overhead. The amount of greenery varies with the owner's commitment—though pottering about an indoor garden has such charms, few people can resist this gentlest of hobbies. But for all sorts of practical reasons, as well as aesthetic ones, there will be a more determined show in the garden room than in the rest of the house. The hose is handy, the tools are probably stored here, as well as all the tonics and medicines healthy plants require. Furnished with a certain style, garden rooms are an almost ideal way to make the most of niggardly sunshine right through the year, if their owners can afford to keep the heating up high enough through the winter months. Allowed to slide, so they become used more for storing garden impedimenta, playpens and paddling pools, they can be melancholy places, full of withered geraniums, and other evidence of past fantasies.

The booming business in ready-made as well as purpose-built glazed house extensions suggests that we are becoming a frankly hedonistic society. Glazed extensions offer a particularly attractive, as well as financially viable way of expanding living space, in urban environments especially. Not that glass houses of this sort are cheap—the purpose-built or architect-designed variety will cost between £10,000 and £20,000—but they are cheaper than bricks and mortar additions as a rule and, more importantly, they connote a glamorous expansion of life style which appeals powerfully to people today. How much more exciting to fit an airy transparent box, dramatic both in sunlight and at night, than a solid one, if one needs space! Architects and designers are equally charmed by the possibilities they offer of tacking a new and unpredictable living space on to pedestrian terrace housing. Glazed extensions can be used ingeniously to fill in the dull dank 'dead space'

Wicker, painted white or left natural, is ideal furniture for indoor/outdoor rooms. It is portable, pretty and makes a nice foil to ebullient greenery and flowers. With a place like this tacked on to a town house, sunny and stacked with growing things, one could be cool about having no view or no garden.

The indoorness moves outdoors here, with the surprising difference that this amazingly vivid and thickly planted spot is high in the sky, a roof garden no less. Striped matting is a kind thought for people who like to sprawl in the sun. I keep wondering how many sacks of compost they had to lug up here.

between back extensions, to house staircases or to convert a sunless courtyard into an intriguing and useful extra room, with romantic lighting dropping through the glazing above. The most ambitious architectural schemes often involve a glazed addition over two floors, with staircase access moved to the new extension thus releasing space inside. Again, not cheap, but possibly cheaper and more fun than simply transferring to a larger house of the same type.

There are snags, of course. One, which even genius architects like Mies van der Rohe have overlooked, is that large glazed areas attract the sun's heat like a magnifying glass, even in temperate climates. His celebrated and beautiful Farnsworth House—more house than garden room but pretty glassy notwithstanding—was a proper little furnace in summer, and this gave rise to considerable litigation between architect and client. Large, glazed areas generate so much more heat when the sun is shining that they either need special ventilation, like glazed panels opening window-fashion or some sort of blind arrangement (louvred blinds usually) that block off some of the ultraviolet. Siting the garden room in a shady, northerly spot guards against this of course, but then you rarely have more than an hour or two of sun each day, and your plants are less flourishing. On the whole, though, unless one is living in a detached residence with walls facing off in every direction, there is not much choice—better a glass oven or a glass shadow box than no glass at all. Keeping the place warm in winter is probably less of a problem than keeping it cool in summer, it just costs more. What glass houses do best, practically speaking, is keep the rain and wind off you when you feel like communing with nature, otherwise they seem more romantic than practical which is, no doubt, their special charm.

The indoors-outdoors half of the equation, whether it is a few chairs on the patio or a table and benches under the wisteria-hung pergola, is idyllic and cheap, while the weather behaves itself. Eating outside on a hot summer's evening, with moths bombarding the candle-shades, and people and foliage black outlines against a fading sky, is one of the most civilized of human pleasures, worth any amount of effort and improvization. It is particularly important in cities. To be able to walk out of a swarming street, gritty and noisy, through a building and out the other side into a charmed bubble of tranquillity, trailing leaves lifted by the breeze, with candles and green scents, is an urban version of going through the looking-glass. Just as wonderful is taking your breakfast and morning paper outside to catch the early morning sun, in high summer, at the hour when the vegetable world around you is still damply new and fragrant.

Human comforts need to be provided for if you are trying for an outdoor experience in a city. Thyme-scented hollows of turf are all one needs on a cliff ramble, but stretching out on even the most expensive form of paving is not relaxing. What estate agents call patios, and architects call paved areas, need as much comfort and softness as you can provide, even if you do have to drag all the cushions inside when it starts raining. Benches, wood, stone, concrete, even bricks cushioned with thyme as at Sissinghurst, are a sturdy component of garden architecture, and look inviting, warmed by the sun. But no one can sit on them comfortably for very long. The sun makes townspeople long to sprawl, strip off, hang out. Those canvas-covered folding recliners are still ugly and badly designed, but they are exactly what the human body craves for on a sultry, sticky afternoon. To eat outside, with any degree of ease, one needs a table and benches or chairs. Outdoor eating places can be romanticized quite easily, with profuse greenery (ivy, in every shade from spinach to the most frivolous variegated varieties, takes a while to get going but rewards handsomely thereafter), tubs of flowers chosen for scent or colour or gaiety, some form of night lighting, ranging from the slightly theatrical hidden spots, casting extravagant shadows, to the simplest glass shaded candles or night lights.

Caring for indoor-outdoor plants should not be a problem since the market is flooded with books on the subject. Any method of watering makes quite a mess. The sensible way to deal with large pots is shift them outdoors, so the water can run away without flooding the floor of the garden room, but this is heavy duty stuff. I find most smaller pot plants respond best to dunking in a bucket of cool—not ice cold—water to which one adds, now and then, a pinch of phostrogen plant food. When the bubbles stop rising the pot is saturated and must then be drained. Even then, as anyone who enjoys having plants around the house will know, a buffer is essential between the pot base and table. Cache pots usually come provided with their own saucer, which looks neater than old plates.

Many indoor plants, like cyclamen or azaleas (these are, of course, also outdoor plants, but I am referring to the hothouse-grown variety which need hardening off if they are going to be put outdoors), look best standing on their own. Others, from geraniums to dramatic foliage, demand more of a massed showing. Here is the rub—finding suitable containers, affordably, is not easy. Flea marketeers come up with surprising solutions. Old hipbaths, for instance, can look magnificently sculptural, painted up inside and out, but they need a really lavish display of plants of differing heights, though this can be faked by propping some up on empty cans. Victorian slop bowls in painted china are—if you can find them—attractive enough to stand about on tables. Cheap plastic tubs and troughs, such as most garden centres stock, do not look at all bad if they are painted a suitably inoffensive colour—grey-green, off-white, even black. A patchwork of Victorian tiles makes a splendid plant trough to stand on an inside windowsill, with herbs or whatever. A handyman or woman could knock one up, using a lipped moulding or picture

Glazed Extensions
Anyone thinking of adding a pre-fabricated glazed extension should look at the *Which?* report published in May 1983. The report lists the pros and cons of different brands, points out details to look out for (louvres v. roof vents for summer ventilation, staging for plants and seed trays) and suggests which are feasible DIY propositions.

Actually it's a bathroom, but a bathroom affiliated to the great outdoors, via glass paned door and the wonderful knubbly texture of grey cobbles which continue outside.

frame moulding to secure the tiles. The inner plastic trough protects the wooden base of the tiled trough from constant dampness, which would rot it away in time. The same goes for any plant container of wood or other perishable material.

The natural location for many plants is under a window, since most of them prefer light. The most attractive plant stands of all time were the Victorian ones in curled wire and metal, but these are almost unfindable today. A possible alternative might be the base of a treadle sewing-machine, cleaned up, with a metal or plastic trough slotted in where the machine used to be. Old metal pot and pan stands, consisting of a tall, slender metal structure with graded apertures for the *batterie de cuisine*, can be made into decorative plant holders, too. Painting them is not the problem here, what is tricky is finding plants of suitably graded size, so the pyramidal shape is roughly maintained. The plant pots, too, must be graded to fit into the apertures and a large tin tray is needed to stand the whole thing on, to catch drips after watering.

THE KNACK

Doing It Yourself

It is easy to make fun of the DIY scene with its manuals and magazines and its 'experts' fixated with fixatives and laminates. I once shared a phone-in with an expert among the experts and listened with bated breath while he counselled a worried lady on the sound-proofing of her loo. I kept my eye on him while he rattled on about acoustic properties and sound-insulating materials, but not a ghost of a grin could I detect on his earnest face.

Shorn of its mystique, however, DIY is an admirable pastime, utterly absorbing, genuinely rewarding, a means for us all of contacting our old childish joys—making mud pies, building sand-castles, creating tents out of blankets and chairs, and dens in hollowed-out shrubberies. It is the gleeful seriousness of it all which is childlike, not the results, which can often be astonishingly sophisticated and professional. There are two things I should emphasize about DIY. First, forestalling all the usual objections, is that you do not know what you are capable of till you try. Second, is that if you try hard you are likely to make a better job than half-hearted professionals simply because you *care* how it turns out.

Know thyself is the maxim to bear in mind. After trying my hand at just about every DIY job from putting in window frames to patching plaster to laying a ring circuit, I now know what I'm good at and where to put my not inconsiderable muscle (nothing like these jobs for muscle building). One is usually best at what one enjoys doing. I hate measuring and tackling a whole new construction—cupboards, shelving, putting up pelmet boards—from scratch; or patiently repeating an operation—like drilling screw holes in a set of shelves—on a table, comfortably seated. To become involved I have to see results almost immediately. I might knock up a cupboard frame and surround—not measuring of course, except with a piece of string—quite fast, and then take weeks to assemble some simple doors. I am not a joiner, nor a bricklayer, nor a plasterer (plastering needs bull-like strength) but I am a patient and persevering restorer. I'll scrape wood, burn off paint, clean old plaster, make good holes in walls or doors, fill, sand and paint any surface as if my life depended on it. When I have time I can prepare, make good, and decorate a room to the highest professional standards.

The jobs I excel at are not ambitious (decorative finishes aside) but they are slow and painstaking, and I do them better. Another person, with different talents, might enjoy planning ring circuits, or working out the plumbing arrangements for a new kitchen or bathroom. Others adore meticulous measuring, drawing up plans or assembling the bits for an elaborate piece of joinery—all that 'offering up' which drives me mad.

Paint, blessedly, is cheap enough to allow a little latitude—if the first layer of sponged-on colour is too bright or too watery, give it another and another still if need be. Stop when the results please you. Don't be put off by making mistakes, or doing it wrong—the only wrong effect in a subjective area like this is the one you don't like. In fact, most mistakes can be retrieved after a pause for reflection. Almost the only absolute rule in the paint finish game is that oil-based paints should be thinned ('let down' is the tradesman's phrase) with white spirit or turpentine; and water-based paints are thinned with water.

Ninety-nine per cent of amateur efforts delight their authors and the only thing inhibiting more people from dabbling in colours and effects is a misplaced, counter-productive fear of going wrong, getting flak from their loved ones or teasing from the workforce. One of my first dragged rooms, in the most intricate shades of red over a pinky base colour, had all my Dorset building team in hysterics, convinced that the tank above had overflowed and mussed up my nice neat paint finish. We all had a good laugh, but I promised them they would eat their words when they saw it in its finished state and, to a large extent, they did.

Old For New & New For Old

Twenty years ago it was still possible to pick up good stuff cheap if you knew where to look and were prepared to do a bit of restoration work. One could buy Regency card-tables, mahogany with brass or ebony inlay, for £20, a whole set of Dickens in half calf for £8.50 or fine old rugs for £15. Alas, those easy pickings are at an end. Perhaps the good stuff is simply running out, perhaps people have become more knowledgeable thanks to the media about the value of their possessions, or perhaps it really is the case that people are buying antiques or attractive junk, who would not have seen the point of it twenty years ago. At any rate you have to be a bit clever and very persistent to light on a real buy or a bargain these days. It can still be done—largely by knowing where to look—but you have to look harder.

Rule one: try the unobvious places. Avoid fashionable city streets lined with antique shops or pretty bow-windowed shops in country towns and villages. Large, bleak, impersonal-looking establishments called Furniture Mart or something of the kind are nearer the bargain mark. They specialize in second hand or nearly new, but often if you poke about discriminatingly you may stumble on a piece with possibilities: funny Victorian chairs with buttoned upholstery hidden under a crude home-made cover; bedroom chairs of decent shape buried in paint, caned seats missing and a piece of ply tacked over; well-made deco or Thirties furniture, its good wood and solid craftsmanship concealed by villainous varnish; a pretty jug, slightly cracked, but nice for flowers; old children's books, with coloured plates. What you are looking for, and it shines out even when it's buried under chipped paint, is quality, some grace or care in the making. With practice you will be able to spot quality at a glance, across a room or a street or a crowded market. I know women who can pick out the one good item on a tumbled stall of jumble, in one predatory second.

The chance of a bargain arises when somebody (shopkeeper or dealer) fails to see the quality of an item, or maybe does not even know what it is, or how special a thing of its type it is, and prices it down. Knowledge helps here, of course, and no time spent in museums, galleries and houses open to the public is wasted—it all hones the eye and makes it more discriminating. You should also leaf through books and magazines, picking up stray information, studying well-documented pieces in full colour. If this sounds like heavy research, I can promise that it isn't to interested parties. I should also say that an eye for quality is trained just as much by looking and comparing, by idle curiosity.

Other unobvious places to search include demolition yards where you might discover bashed-about lead garden urns or a stained-glass window or tiled grate, vastly cheaper than in architectural salvage establishments though these too are worth checking out. If there is one in your locality, it pays to drop in often on the off-chance—the same is true for any of the places mentioned. Who knows? Today's barren waste may blossom into bargain country overnight as the result of a house clearance or a local private sale. If you are not proud, a quick rummage in skips can produce amazing finds—a neighbour found an eighteenth-century chair, minus one leg, in a local skip. That makes it rubbish to the *ignoranti*, but the *cognoscenti* know full well that the value of an eighteenth-century chair amply justifies paying a cabinet-maker to copy the missing leg. Rural tips are forbidden to scavengers (I did say you must swallow your pride) but most country districts have unofficial dumps, somewhere out in no-man's-land, where all sorts of useful and promising, if not antique, finds can be made. Jolly old wirelesses, laundry baskets, moquette-covered armchairs, Thirties style and in scabrous condition, but salvageable.

Rule two: Obvious places are worth trying if you know how to use them. Auctions and salerooms are haunted by dealers and the good stuff is not usually given away. Standard items will be cheapest there, making them ideal venues for bulky sofas, cupboards, kitchen tables, rolls of second-hand carpet, old curtains, velvet or damask, all faded or worn. Street markets—search out the less fashionable ones and go really early, around dawn—display what looks like the scourings of a thousand cellars and attics on their stalls but, somewhere in there, there is always a pearl or two. With unfashionable Brick Lane on my doorstep, I take it in most Sundays and it has largely furnished and tricked out a large house for me. Sometimes it is an eighteenth-century print in its original frame but minus glass ('It's old, love, you can see it's old. Yours for a fiver.'), sometimes a little Thirties armchair with down-filled cushions, sometimes a set of Provençal pottery plates. You should always haggle a bit to show you know the form, but settle before they get exasperated.

Old textiles are the best buy these days, where the real coups can be made, if you have an eye for the authentic or special. This could be a set of old lace panels, machine made but wonderfully floriferous, a length of hand-printed silk never made up, a linen velvet cushion cover, dirty and cobbled together but glowing where the light catches it. If you take a fancy to something particular, it is worth chatting to the dealers to find out where they buy. Patrons of street markets should keep an open mind and a reluctant purse—it's so easy, having made the trip there, to feel you can't go back empty handed. In that mood, one falls for the blarney, pays too much for something one doesn't really covet. On the other hand, know by the pricking of your thumbs when the really tremendous buy presents itself, and then just go out and buy it.

Power Tools

What about power tools? Experience suggests that the most expensive of these, the heavy-duty type, are so much the best that it would be better to borrow or hire what you need. DIY versions, in comparison, are toys, under-powered so that you spend ages trying to drill a brick or cut a curved pelmet with a dolly-size jig. Powerful tools make you handier, too, but for heaven's sake be careful.

A bench saw, slicing up wood like cheese, is a great invention but costs hundreds. Ordinary hand-saws cut up most domestic-sized planks and timbers, if you get them sharpened regularly. Don't do this yourself—many DIY and most tool shops get it done for you.

RECOGNIZING QUALITY

The quality I am talking about here is not expert knowledge, the trained eye which can date or attribute a painting by a scrutiny of the brushstrokes, even though I love reading about Rembrandts discovered on street stalls. Who doesn't? The recognizing faculty I mean is more instinctive, less specialized, but as keen as the truffle hound's nose for a buried tuber. Any treasures to be found today will probably have to be unearthed, too, metaphorically speaking. Look carefully at any item daubed in cheap, chipped paint. If it is shapely or comely, test it further. Pick it up—weight is a crude index of age. A well-made old thing usually has a sort of massiveness, wood was thicker, glass was heavier, metals solid rather than hollowed. Look at the construction and detail. Well-made drawers, solid brass handles, brass feet with castors—all these indicate furniture worthy of money spent on extras.

Crude over-painting can hide beautiful gilt mirror or picture frames, pretty Victorian scrap screens. I bought a screen in a furniture market because I had a hunch that it held some secret. It cost me all of £2. Sure

What to Tackle
Certain DIY tasks are best left to the professionals. One is plastering, ceilings especially. The other is bricklaying, which, like pastry-making or breadmaking, flows from ease and familiarity—without the knack it takes too long and looks clumsy.

Physical work, which DIY is, needs to find a rhythm to go well, fast and efficiently. Try to allow enough time—a week of evenings, one weekend clear—to finish a job you have started. Rope in friends or paid helpers (young school leavers, or students on holiday are invaluable—try to pay them cash at the end of the day) if necessary. A stop-go situation is bad—it means you lose the knack, it all becomes unfamiliar and hard work again, and you put off little finishing touches for weeks when you may have got the basics together in days.

enough, under the loathsome wallpaper and pink enamel paint, was a pretty, nostalgic nursery screen, with scraps arranged to make pictures and a surround of varnished pine. There was also a small hole, smack through one panel, and, of course, it was that hole that got me my bargain because somebody stuck the wallpaper on to hide it and then painted the frame pink to match. Nearly all my best finds were overpainted. Removing the paint can be a problem or a torment, if it is what it often is today—a couple of coats of standard emulsion, which resists every known solvent. If it is valuable enough and you care enough, you will manage somehow, even if it means scraping it off inch by inch with a scalpel. A form of mild insanity perhaps, but childishly rewarding.

REFURBISHING AND RESTORING
Half the fun of buying junk is getting it home again and cleaning it up. Cleaning up in many cases *is* restoring. More elaborate restoration—cabinet work, mending and over-painting china or re-upholstery is outside the scope of this book and indeed that of most people unless they are prepared to study the craft, buy tools and equipment and launch into a full-scale hobby. Always bear in mind, if you find something fragile and possibly valuable, that you should take it to an expert for identification before doing anything to it other than blow off the dust.

FURNITURE
Nearly all junky furniture was given a French polish or similar finish. Over the years this gets stained, grimy and darkened until the wood grain is scarcely visible. I usually try to get it off because this reveals the honest wood again, and because anything but the most expert French polishing is inferior to bare wood oiled or waxed. Roughly speaking, mahogany was usually French polished; most other woods were given some sort of varnish stain to darken them and give them a shine. French polish dissolves in methylated spirits, but the varnishes must be removed with paint stripper. The procedure in both cases is the same. Remove all encumbrances like handles, knobs and hinges if possible.

Materials
You will need a large can of paint stripper or a litre bottle of methylated spirits (get some of each if you are not certain what you are dealing with). Have two rolls of wire wool, medium and fine grades, a pair of tough rubber gloves, soft cloths and lots of newspaper. You may also need linseed oil, wax polish, white spirit or turpentine, wood stain, plastic wood or brummer stopping and grain filler: check the methods and your piece of furniture to see which of these you will want.

Method
This work is best tackled outside to dissipate the fumes. Spread the newspaper around to catch the mess and work on one area of a piece at a time.

To remove French polish, swab the wood with methylated spirits, then begin rubbing with medium wire wool. In a moment or two the polish begins to soften and can be wiped off. You may need to repeat this once or twice to get it smooth and clean—stickiness means some polish or softened shellac remains. After the last application, use fine wire wool and rub in the direction of the wood grain. This sleeks and polishes it dramatically, so keep using clean handfuls of wire wool. When the piece is clean and silky, wipe it to remove filaments of wire wool, then rub in boiled linseed oil thinned in two to one proportions with white spirit or real turpentine. Do this several times in the course of a week and the rich natural colour will revive and a mild shine return. For more shine, just rub away with soft cloths.

Any parts of the piece which turn out to be a different colour—or even a different wood, which is not infrequent in cheaper furniture—can be stained to match the rest, using a proprietary wood stain, which is simply wiped on with a soft cloth till the right tone is reached. This beauty treatment works as well on mahogany veneer as on solid wood, but take care if patches of veneer are lifting or loose. They should be glued and cramped back before cleaning begins. Stray missing bits can be either neatly patched with new veneer; or filled with plastic wood or brummer stopping which must then be sanded back and stained to match the rest; or bodged over by staining the pale wood carcase beneath to make the patch less obvious.

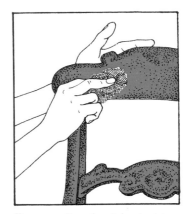

To remove French polish rub with wire wool soaked in methylated spirits.

To remove old varnish or varnish and stain the procedure is exactly the same, except that you use paint stripper which you should take care not to get on your skin—it stings painfully and should be splashed immediately with cold water. The varnish tends to be thicker and stickier so you will need to renew the wire wool frequently. If the wood is pale and fine grained—beech, ash, pine or deal—you will probably want to keep it that way. A light oiling with linseed oil, as above, followed by waxing, will bring it up nicely. Pieces that get a lot of handling or kicking, like chair legs, can be given two coats of clear polyurethane varnish to seal and protect the wood, but rub these down lightly with fine sandpaper or wire wool when the varnish is dry to dull the shine.

Oak, which is a biscuit colour in its natural state but darkens through gingery brown to black in time, is a special case which may need different treatment. Prolonged rubbing with wire wool and stripper will get the surface back to the original shade, though some varnish will remain in the coarse open grain of the wood. To keep it pale, you first need to fill the grain, then seal and wax as above. Proprietary grain filler, which is white, powdery plastery stuff, can be bought from specialist woodworking shops. Follow the instructions and stain the whole area with light oak stain (to colour the filler to match the wood) before sealing. A similar effect is achieved by painting on acrylic gesso (which you buy from art shops), tinted with acrylic paint to a natural wood colour, then sanding or wire woolling when dry to clear the wood and leave gesso in the grain only. Easier still, paint over the whole piece with undercoat tinted to a pale biscuit and rub over with a rough cloth while still tacky to clear the wood. When the colour pleases you, seal, then wax to protect it and give it a mild sheen. Painting on lines, with fine brush and oil colour mixed into thinned varnish, can be used to jazz up the look of squarish simple pieces, like desks and cupboards. Do this before sealing.

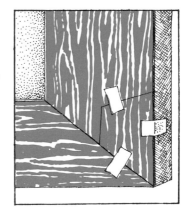

Slide glue under loose veneer and patch, press down and tape into position till set.

The same filling trick can be used, more dramatically, if the oak is coloured or stained first. Yves St. Laurent works at one such elegant, plain, Japanese-looking oak desk. First the bare wood is stained black with wood stain. Then filler is applied all over and the surface rubbed clear before the filler sets hard to leave it in the grain only. White filler in blackened wood gives a chic, charcoal grey look to the wood, which is then sealed and waxed as above. You can use strong colours, like dark red or green for a more striking result.

METALWORK
Rust, corrosion, dirt or the years' thick tarnish, obscure most metal objects, from grates to locks. The first step is to give them a tentative cleaning to see what further needs doing. Rusty iron is brushed with a wire brush; proprietary rust remover should be swabbed on next, following instructions;

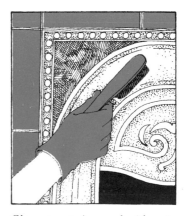

Clean up rusty iron work with a wire brush.

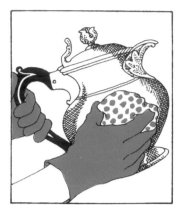

Silverware can be safely polished with Silvo or jeweller's rouge.

and further cleaning is done with coarse or medium grade wire wool. When the metal is clean and bright, it will need protecting against future rust or corrosion. A proprietary spray, called WD 40 and obtainable at cycle shops, is excellent for this. I spray it liberally over any metal object which looks time worn.

Metal kept indoors can be burnished beautifully with old-fashioned grate polish. Outdoors, it needs red lead primer, followed by oil-based paint and varnish. Metal with moving parts, rusted or jammed, can be eased by soaking in penetrating oil, then cleaning bit by bit with fine sandpaper and cloths. Fancy locks and clockwork may need expert attention. Old brass and copper can be cleaned up more speedily by soaking in ordinary vinegar to which a very little spirits of salt is added. Dry carefully, then rub with very fine grade wire wool. Finish with standard metal polish. A buffer pad attachment on an electric drill brings brass and copper up to a brilliant polish. Silver and silver plate only need patient polishing, using Silvo or jeweller's rouge.

NEW FURNITURE
Relatively speaking, cheap new furniture is more expensive than the equivalent junk piece. Sometimes, though, one needs a piece of a specific size or type—kitchen units, bedside cabinets, a child's desk. Again, you may have inherited some of that knotty deal which was fashionable a few years ago and which has become grimy and scuffed. You may have acquired built-in shelves and cupboards with your house or flat and these have the crude finish and harsh texture of bodged-up joinery. All these items can be made much more attractive and expensive looking by refinishing properly, with paint or varnish stains and, in some cases, with painted decoration or applied mouldings.

REFINISHING
The method you use varies according to how you want the piece to look. Pieces to be revarnished, or stained and varnished, need to have any old seal or varnish removed, with stripper and wire wool (see *Furniture*, pages 144–145). Knotty deal, I think, looks better given a colourful varnish stain—Dulux have some excellent colours, which deepen the more coats you apply. This helps fade out those knots and gives the piece a folksy, Scandinavian look, which you can emphasize further by painted lines or stencilled patterns—great for kitchen or nursery stuff. Try to do any varnishing in a dust-free atmosphere and go over the surface after each coat with fine wet-and-dry abrasive paper used with soapy water to soften the cutting action. This gives that deliciously silky surface which is part of the appeal of high-class painted furniture. All varnished work is improved by meticulous rubbing down.

A repeated stencilled pattern can put the finishing touch to nursery furniture.

Old kitchen units have an extra tough finish, which is next to impossible to remove. If badly chipped and cracked, the best way to renovate this is to fill the damaged parts carefully using brummer stopping, which dries smooth and hard. Sand it level with the surface, then sand the whole unit to roughen the surface a little and provide a key for paint. Paint with undercoat, then two coats of gloss or eggshell, which is less shiny. The important thing is to smooth each coat when dry with fine sandpaper to remove grit, nibs and runs and give a level surface for the next coat. If you work at this and varnish carefully at the end, you will contrive a finish nearer to fine, hard paint than plastic, but it will look all the better for that. If you are in an experimental mood, consider tarting up those flat unit doors. Huge Letraset lettering—CROCKS, SPICES, PANS—looks impressively graphic and shows where things belong besides. Mondrian-like coloured squares and lines can be achieved by marking out the area with sticky tape and painting between,

Use big Letraset lettering to cheer up unit doors.

though the sticky residue is not easy to clean off. Stencils offer enormous variety, from neat all-over patterns to one large motif and are great fun to do (see *Stencils*, pages 171–172).

New whitewood or built-in units, with doors of ply or blockboard, usually need the actual texture improved as the wood is coarse grained, gritty and unpleasant to handle. Painting is a necessary disguise, I think, but first the actual wood needs filling to refine the surfaces. The easiest way to do this is to paint the whole surface with a watery mix of Polyfilla using a large brush, working it well in across the grain. Or, if you have it to hand and the piece is not too large, use acrylic gesso, which has a harder finish and dries more quickly. When dry, sand thoroughly to force the filler into the wood grain and leave a clean surface. It may need a second application, sanded as before. While sanding, pay attention to the corners of doors, the legs of tables and any other sharp edges. Smoothing, even slightly rounding these off, makes them look and feel infinitely better. What you are aiming for is a fine, hard, even surface, which is the best base to paint on. Having got that, apply the undercoat. Sand, then apply a split-coat, half undercoat, half eggshell or gloss. This is an old-fashioned painter's method, which I swear by, as it gives a tougher final finish. Sand again, then apply, as smoothly as possible, a final coat of top coat—on the whole eggshell is better on the humbler woods, as it shows up unevennesses less, and is a kindly texture to live with. Perfectionists may give two final coats.

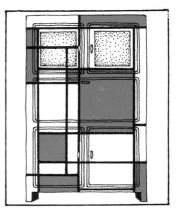

A striking Mondrianesque effect can be achieved by painting between lines of sticky tape.

DECORATION

Now, decoration. Modern whitewood furniture is so bland it can do with a little surface interest. The prettiest finish I have arrived at was an all-over stencilled pattern based on an Indian calico print. Slow, but the kind of thing one can do in spare moments, bit by bit. Use signwriter's paints or acrylic colours which dry almost instantly to prevent smudging (see *Stencils*, pages 171–172). Sponging colour on is another easy way for non-painters to decorate. It looks pretty with a painted line trim. You can sponge with one colour, or two, or several, for a marbled look. Use watered-down acrylic paint or, for a softer effect, the standard decorative paint mix—1 tablespoon white undercoat or eggshell thinned to milky consistency with approximately ½ pint (300 ml) white spirit, and tinted with artists' oil colours. Use a natural sponge and take up a very small amount of the colour each time—dab it on a piece of paper first to check it won't splatter. The sort of colour mix which sponging lends itself to might be over, say, white or off-white, a light sponging in beige-grey; over this, when dry, a light sponging in shrimp pink; over this, when dry, a wide-spaced sponging in coral; paint any line trim in coral.

Built-in cupboard doors, once painted decently, can be decorated to go with the wall finish, which makes them a lot less dreary, almost invisible in

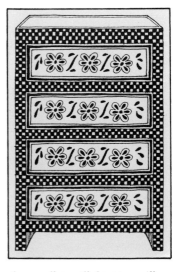

An overall stencilled pattern will transform otherwise bland whitewood furniture.

Detail of the stencil used on the previous page.

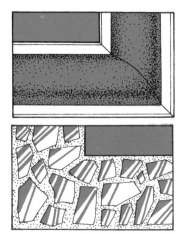

Brighten up a dingy print by rubbing over with a slice of bread.

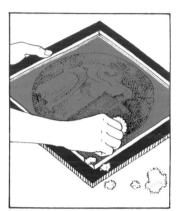

Four finishes for mirror frames: velvet (top) mosaic (above), sea shell (centre) and lace with silk flowers (far right).

fact. I stencilled the same pattern on the sliding doors of a bathroom cupboard as on the walls, and this made a comparatively enormous cupboard shrink visually to pull the whole room together. Alternatively, those great flat expanses can be broken up decoratively in various ways. On hinged doors, mouldings can be tacked and glued on to suggest panelling, then the panel centres can be painted a different tone from the surrounds. The same thing can be suggested with painted lines (see pages 166–167) and a criss-cross trellis pattern looks elegant inside a solid painted border. A tiny overall stencil is a possibility but one needs the patience of a saint to cover a large area.

PICTURES, PRINTS AND FRAMES

Any oil painting with a hint of style or skill should be shown to an expert these days. Apart from a tentative wipe over with a damp cloth, I feel any cleaning is best done by professionals, expensive but justified if you consider the painting has merit.

Prints can be considerably improved by dusting, then rubbing gently all over with a slice of bread, crust removed. This takes off surface grime. Some marks will come off with a very soft eraser, used carefully so as not to rub away the paper. Flymarks or old stains can be bleached away by professionals (most framers will do this) to give an as-new brightness. They can also repair tears and holes invisibly though this costs a bit. On reflection, however, you might find you like your print a little time stained. A new mount will tidy it up considerably, and make the ageing look intentional.

Cutting mounts is something one can learn to do competently oneself. It is surprising what a difference a good mount makes to all sorts of lesser artwork—little watercolours and old photos, as well as prints and maps. Old frames, which I buy whenever I see them going cheap, can often hold photos and prints if you bridge the gap with a mount cut to fit both. Ideally, frame and mount should echo the shape of the picture, with a slightly larger area beneath. Of course, one can bend these rules—if the walls are bare and you ache to liven them up, a slightly mis-mated frame and picture is better than nothing at all. Very small pictures are often given importance by framing in relatively large frames.

MOUNTS

Old frames should be prepared by removing old brads and tacks with pincers or pliers, thoroughly cleaning and polishing up the glass or getting new glass cut. Most art shops will do this cheaply for you. Wipe over with a soapy rag to clean, back and front. Gilt frames should be cleaned cautiously, as gold leaf is tissue thin. A vinegar-water solution, swabbed on with cotton wool is safe and effective. Old discoloured varnish, often applied over gold leaf, can be removed very cautiously, with advantage, but you may take off a little gold here and there. I use paint stripper, painted on with a soft brush then wiped off, bit by bit, with cotton wool.

With the frame prepared, take the inside rebate measurements for the mounting card. Mounting card can be bought from most artist supply shops. It comes in many colours and with a textured Ingres paper finish as well as plain. Brightly-coloured mounts suit some modern prints and jolly-up things like maps and woodcuts but, on the whole, safe neutrals, from off-white to cream or buff, are best and one tires of them less. It is worth dropping in to a good framer's or an interior decorator's, and studying the professional approach to similar things. Clever, quite elaborate, mounts using marbled paper, inked lines, bands washed in soft colours, or the narrowest gold strips undoubtedly lift a modest print into a different class. This takes time and practice, though, and is most effective where a set of prints are being dealt with and matching frames make a considered grouping on a wall.

Materials
To cut mounts, you will need a scalpel or Stanley knife, a darning needle, a steel rule, a sharp pencil and a sheet of glass with taped edges or scrap ply to cut on.

Method
Pencil the rebate measurements of the frame on the card, but rule it $\frac{1}{16}$ inch (2 or 3 mm) smaller all round to allow leeway and accommodate any non-right-angled corners on the frame. Cut straight through with the knife blade. Now position your print, map or photo on the cut mount, checking that it is equidistant from both sides and the top, but a little further from the bottom edge. Prick all four corners through into the mount with a darning needle to indicate where the 'window' is to be cut. Old prints and engravings with a raised edge all round, showing where the paper was stamped, should be mounted to display this. Any lettering below should also be revealed, either by extending the 'window' downwards, or by cutting out a separate little 'window', which looks professional and elegant but adds to your problems. With a pencil, rule faintly and clearly between the pin pricks. Check that the 'window' is right-angled at all corners, correcting as necessary.

Now for the cutting. Traditionally, windows are bevelled at a 45° angle, which sets off the artwork neatly, looks professional and echoes the inward slope of most picture frames. The sloping edge of a steel rule helps one to cut at the correct angle without wobbling. I tend to hold my breath, press the blade in and slice away bravely in one swift, steady movement. Using a new blade, the card can normally be cut through in one go, though you may need to ease the blade into the corners again to give a neat mitred angle. Some people have the knack for cutting neatly, and straight—if you simply cannot, I would give up the bevelled edge and cut straight through using the steel rule to guide the blade.

When the window is cut, fix the print in place with a small piece of sticky tape on all four sides, then lay it on the immaculately clean glass in the frame, replace the backing (or cut new backing from thick card) and tap in brads all round with a tack hammer. It is best to do this with the frame laid on a soft blanket and a heavy weight along the side you are hammering into. Then cover the back with brown paper, held down all round with gummed strip, screw in rings, and wire up securely.

There are many ways of grouping pictures attractively or of making more of them with ribbon, cords and, painted loops (see page 121).

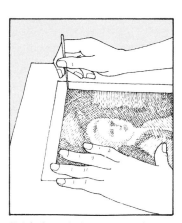

Prick through the corners with a darning needle to indicate the area to be cut out.

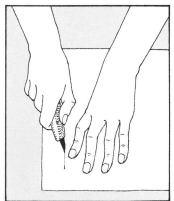

Use a new blade to cut a bevelled edge.

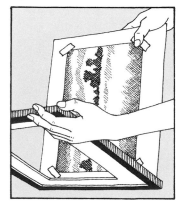

Hold the print in position with sticky tape on the corners.

Trace off old prints for penwork decoration, or design your own, like this domino pattern.

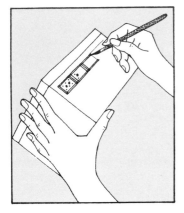

Indian ink, a mapping pen and a steady hand are the basic equipment for penwork.

PENWORK

Small wooden things—boxes, trays, lamp bases, frames—can be given an utterly unexpected and charming appearance by decorating them all over with Indian ink and a mapping pen. This makes them look a little like carved ivory or those engraved and inked whale tooth ornaments called scrimshaw. This is another lady's hobby, popular in the late eighteenth and nineteenth centuries. Using engravings or pattern books as inspiration, amateurs produced some exquisite trifles, eagerly sought after by dealers today for their delicacy and charm. The Victoria and Albert Museum in London has a stunning penwork bureau, and I have seen several small cupboards with this filigree-like decoration. Here is my own method of penworking.

Materials

You will need acrylic gesso and a good quantity of sandpaper for the initial preparation stages. Equip yourself with orange shellac, methylated spirits, brushes, mapping pens, Indian ink and carbon paper. Use clear varnish to finish.

Method

First smooth the piece by sanding it all over, then give enough coats of acrylic gesso to build up a hard, fine, china-like surface. Sand again, then brush on two coats of orange shellac, thinned one to one with methylated spirits. This will instantly colour the white gesso ivory-yellow as well as sealing it and making it extra smooth. Most penwork pieces have repeating borders of the classical motif type, containing central panels representing quite elaborate scenes modelled on engravings—*The Three Graces*, *The Judgment of Paris*, *Cupid and Psyche*. I see no shame in copying either, even tracing off the main outlines through carbon. After that, you simply get out your mapping pens and Indian ink and set to work under a good overhead light. Indian ink dries instantly so smudging is not a problem. Mistakes are best corrected by painting out with more gesso and shellac, not rubbing off. The odd slip won't show, though, and the total effect is really and truly charming. On completion, varnish all over to protect.

SILHOUETTES

The basis of a silhouette is a recognizable profile, which can then be blacked in with Indian ink, and titivated with hats, curls, bows or whatever you feel suits the character and appearance of the subject. The traditional way to get a profile accurately was to cast a shadow on to a sheet of white paper, posing the subject on a chair at a slight distance from the paper and shining a strong light from a table a couple of yards away. One then traced round the shadow directly on to the paper. The problem with this is that the profile is life size, whereas silhouette pictures look most attractive in miniature, though it is not difficult to get a photographic reproduction made a great deal smaller to whatever size you want. Easier perhaps is simply to take a profile snap, making sure the subject is sitting silhouetted against the light for sharp definition. This can be traced off with fine paper, using a sharp pencil, and then transferred to the plain white card of the silhouette with carbon paper. Using a mapping pen and Indian ink, outline the profile very carefully and fill in with a small brush dipped in the same ink. Added detail should be very fine, like spidery handwriting, or bold in outline, like sailor hats, hairbows, so that the whole silhouette reads at a glance as both a likeness of the subject and an attractive composition.

The virtuoso silhouette makers used to snip their delicate little portraits out of black paper with curved scissors, freehand. These were then pasted

A silhouette taken from a profile snap, traced on to card and filled in with Indian ink.

down on to card. Sometimes the black silhouettes were touched in with fine lines of white, suggesting curls, jewellery, fichu, rather than the features themselves which remained simply black. Most museums, many stately homes, have silhouette paintings to look at for more ideas, and the nineteenth-century mania for hobbies produced charming family groups. Small plain gilt oval frames are available in most artist's supply shops cheaply and framed silhouettes make wonderful presents.

LACQUER

Classic oriental lacquer or '*lac de Chine*' is made by brushing on innumerable coats (at least forty) of the sap of a sub-tropical tree, with much patient and sensitive smoothing and burnishing in between, using substances like powdered stag horn and wood ash. A home-made version of the modern professional method uses spray paint or brushed-on paint, but with much smoothing in between. I recommend final varnishing, even over gloss paint, because gloss varnish enriches colours and well rubbed down gives a tough surface with a soft rather than dazzling shine. As with all superfine paint finishes, patience and time are the key to success.

To give period style and a lively shape add a hat or some other detail that flatters the sitter.

Materials

You will need primer, undercoat, standard and fine surface Polyfilla, glass-paper in medium and fine grades, flourpaper or fine wet-and-dry paper, eggshell or flat oil-based paint *or* cellulose spray paints as sold in garages for car repairs, clear gloss polyurethane varnish, thinner or solvent (white spirits for varnish and oil-based paint), cellulose thinner for spray paint, pumice powder or scouring powder, soap, rags.

Method

First meticulously prime, fill with standard Polyfilla, undercoat, fill with fine surface Polyfilla. Rub down in the direction of the wood grain using medium-grade paper till smooth everywhere, then brush carefully. It may need under-coating again. Then give several coats of oil-based paint, thinning each application with white spirit (approximately 1 part spirit to 6 paint—more thin coats are better than fewer thick ones in the super painting world) brushing out smoothly, and rubbing down when dried hard with medium paper for the first couple of coats and fine paper for the next. When the paint colour is opaque and even and the texture as smooth as china, apply varnish. For spray paints, follow the can directions, holding the can vertically after a minute's shaking, and trying to keep the spray fine and even to avoid runs. Again, rub down between coats once the paint has dried hard. Rigging up a plastic sheet overhead helps to prevent dust settling on the wet paint, but take care with fumes—spray paints in particular are toxic if inhaled freely.

Varnishing follows the same principle—thin the coats a little, brush out as smoothly as possible with a special varnish brush (finer bristles) and rub down with fine grade wet-and-dry paper dampened and rubbed over a bar of soap. This lubricates the cutting action of the paper. Always let varnish coats dry hard—check the maker's instructions. The more thin coats of varnish you apply the nearer the final texture is to real lacquer, but expect the base colour to darken somewhat. For final rubbing down use a professional's trick and make up a soft paste of pumice powder (cabinetwork or furniture trade suppliers) or scouring powder, with water or oil, and gently rub this over the surface with a soft rag, adding more water or oil to lubricate. Wipe this off with a damp cloth and you have a satiny texture with a glow rather than a shine, which is a lovely thing to see and touch and improves the look of any piece of furniture.

Fanciful Fabrics

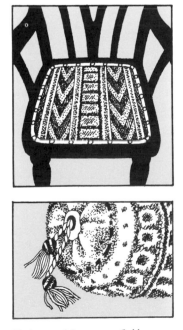

Using invisible thread stitch sheer net to the back of torn lace to repair and strengthen it.

Undamaged fragments of old rugs make stylish covers for chair seats and bolster cushions.

TEXTILES

Cleaning methods for textiles vary according to the type of material or fibres, whether it is embroidered or not and how fragile it looks. If you are in any doubt, take it to a specialist dry cleaner—especially when there is any chance the colours might bleed, as often happens with embroidery silks or cottons. The same goes for pile fabrics, like velvet, chenille and delicate silk damask. All tapestry or needlework needs professional cleaning.

However, that still leaves quite a lot that you can do at home. Anything linen or cotton can be tackled successfully. Do any repairs first, though, because the gentlest washing tends to exacerbate tears and rips. Use sheer net and transparent polyester thread to mend torn lace or embroidery. The net goes on behind to act as a backing and is then stitched in place; torn edges are secured with the invisible thread. White things can be whitened by steeping for an hour in a bucket of cold water to which a tablespoonful of bleach is added. Handwash next and dry out in the sun where possible. Actual stains can be faded by an application of oxalic acid crystals, just wetted with water and applied locally. Repeat this process several times and then wash out. A light starching, preferably with old-fashioned Robin starch, improves most whites. Parchment-coloured lace should not be bleached because this ageing adds to its beauty. Conversely, crudely white, modern cotton lace can be made more attractive by dipping in strong tea (tea leaves removed, of course) to mellow the colour. Any delicate-looking lace—collar, mats or whatever—should really be mounted on white scrap fabric and stretched over a frame before washing.

Old rugs are always improved by shaking and beating to loosen the dust. Damp tea leaves rubbed in and then hoovered up will remove more dust and brighten the colours. Unless the rug is valuable or very fragile, I usually go over it with proprietary carpet shampoo, rubbing the foam in with a sponge and then off again with an old towel. This removes a good deal of the grease and grime. Valuable items need professional attention—expensive but worth it.

Cheaper rugs, or rugs so worn that you can't contemplate spending money on them, can be strengthened and to some extent repaired at home. Holes, rips and weak spots should be patched with hessian or canvas glued on behind with Copydex. Fraying edges are best over-stitched with wool. The same process should be used on fraying ends though here you can usually manage only a holding operation to stop loose ends being sucked into the vacuum cleaner. If rugs are going straight on to hard wood or stone floors, an underlay of felt or foam will prolong their life. Beautiful but fragile rugs are best hung on the wall. Back the rug with canvas to even out the weight, then stitch webbing along the top, sew rings to it and hook these over a wall batten. Fragments of old rugs, unless priceless, can be used to cover stools, chairs or cushions, which always looks magnificent.

FABRICS ON FURNITURE

Some pieces of furniture—simple straight-legged coffee tables, stools, hall tables—lend themselves to covering all over with fabric. This not only unifies the piece visually and hides any defects in finish and joinery, but gives the *frisson* of unexpected texture added to colour. Sealed with two or three coats of clear varnish, for gloss and protection, this always looks millionairish. Choose a fabric with texture, like linen or cotton, not too coarse or loosely woven. Checks, stripes and subtle patterns look good.

Materials

You will need your chosen fabric, wood filler, medium-grain sandpaper, shellac, acrylic gesso, animal glue size (as sold for decorating) and brushes for applying these. You should also have to hand some scissors for trimming, soft cloths for smoothing out wrinkles and some Evostick. For final varnishing, use clear eggshell polyurethane.

Method

Start by giving the piece several coats of acrylic gesso to make it quite smooth. Fill any cracks or holes in the wood and then sand all over. Now coat with shellac, which dries instantly, to seal. Make up some glue size and apply it liberally over the table surfaces. Press the fabric pieces, cut to roughly fit with some turnback or overlap at joins, on to the wet size, one area at a time. Brush more size over and smooth down. The adept will cut the whole cloth cover in one, but I find joins where table top cover meets table leg cover scarcely show. Overlap the fabric on the legs fractionally or you may get a lumpy seam. When dry, you will find it has shrunk taut and tight. Trim off any surplus and stick down any loose bits with Evostik. When quite dry, varnish with clear eggshell polyurethane.

The same technique, using lush fabrics, like plush, velvet or satin, can be used to transform plain mirror and picture frames but use Copydex rather than size, which might stain the fabric. These can be made more gorgeous still by glueing on tarnished silver braid or lace, tassels, little bows or artificial flowers.

SKIRTED TABLES

Skirted tables look deliciously pretty but need not be tables at all according to the dictionary definition. Circles of blockboard standing on tea chests are excellent as sofa tables. But first they need a thick underskirt like an old army

When covering furniture with glued-on fabric leave a little overlap where you need to make joins.

A fabric-covered table finished with several coats of a polyurethane varnish.

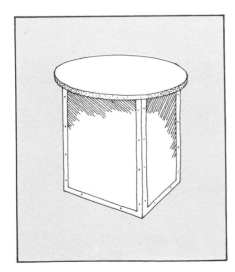

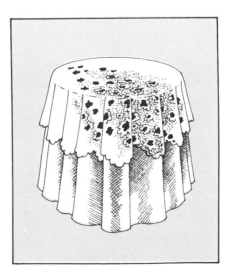

A circular chipboard top propped on a tea chest forms the underpinning for a cheap sofa table—shown here underskirted with an old blanket to give shape to a cotton overskirt, under a scalloped cloth.

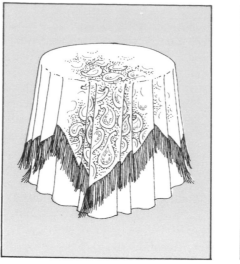

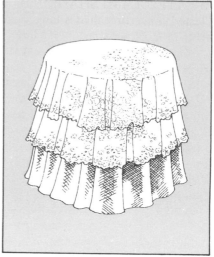

Variations on the skirted table theme: a Paisley shawl (right) or layers of lace cloths (far right) for an easy touch of glamour.

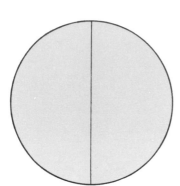

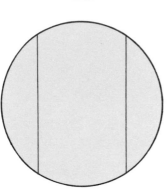

Avoid a centre seam when joining fabric for table covers (top). Two seams (above) make it lie smoothly.

blanket shaped over and trimmed right around at floor level. On top of that goes a topskirt of plain or printed fabric, preferably cotton so it can be easily washed. The skirt should have its hem turned up all round. This can be machined with lace, fringe or bobble fringe (inviting to pets) stitched as a bottom trim.

There are some niceties to consider in the sewing, like where to seam it if the fabric is too narrow. A seam which falls in the centre of the table will form an unsightly ridge. Instead, make two seams, giving a broad central panel which will lie flat.

On top of this, smart tables dress up a stage further with printed floral second skirts, scalloped by machine, or old paisley shawls draped carelessly, fringe trailing. Alternatively, the second skirt could be lots of lacy tea cloths starched like frilly drawers. By now they are so grand they may need a circle of glass or perspex on top to protect them from damage.

RENAISSANCE-TYPE DRAPED TABLES

Cover any uninteresting oblong table which is a good height and size to stand under a window or behind a sofa to make it into a Renaissance extravaganza. Drape the table with an old blanket then cover it with chenille cloth, fabric to match the curtains or an Indian print. This gets rid of the legs, looks distinguished and takes no time. Old rugs look best of all used in this way, as in Renaissance paintings where fascinating still-lifes are created using fruit, perhaps, or musical instruments.

Cover any junk table, first with an old blanket (to give shape) then with a printed fabric or chenille and you have an instantly urbane piece of furniture.

154

PLEATED LAMPSHADES

Pleated concertina shades look stylish and give a warm light especially when made of fabric-covered card. They suit table tops as well as standard lamps.

Materials

You will need large sheets of light, but stiff, card obtainable from artists' supply shops, a ruler clearly marked, a sharp pencil, a paper knife or something else to crease folds, and a punch (like a leather punch). You will, naturally, also have your fabric to cover the card, 1 metre grosgrain ribbon, a wire lampshade frame and some spray-on adhesive which dries clear.

Method

First measure the bottom circumference of the frame, then the vertical struts. You need a rectangle of card twice the length of the circumference and 2 inches (5 cm) longer than the struts the other way. Cut this out with a sharp knife. If the card is not long enough, glue another piece on, stapling for extra strength. Pleats just under 1 inch (2 cm) deep, are right for most shades. With the ruler mark out both sides of card, rule across with a pencil and pleat concertina fashion, first one way, then another, smoothing any creases hard

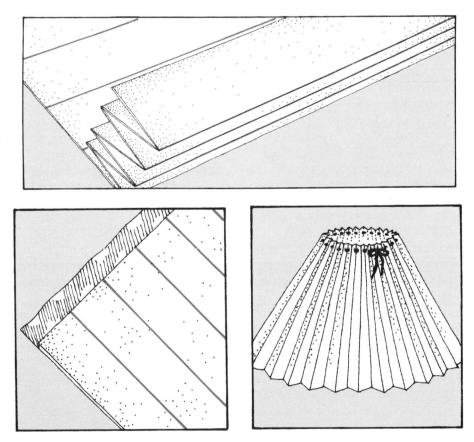

To make a pleated lampshade, first cut your card to size, then pleat concertina fashion (top); spray card with adhesive and lay over fabric leaving a $\frac{1}{2}$ inch (1.2 cm) turnback (far left); punch holes, thread drawstring and tighten to fit wire frame (left).

with the knife. When complete, open out and tack flat again. Spray adhesive on to the card. Lay the fabric flat, cut with half-inch (1 cm) turnbacks top and bottom and spray that with adhesive, too. Using a helper to keep them aligned, stick the fabric down and press out flat. Turn back the edges.

With the punch at its widest setting, make a hole in centre of each pleat approx. 1–1¼ inches (2–3 cm) from the edge. Re-pleat the card, to make folds through the fabric cover. Overlap the ends of the shade by $\frac{1}{2}$ inch (1 cm) and glue, pegging till dry. Thread the ribbon through the holes, draw up and adjust to sit over the wire frame.

Perfect Paint Finishes

PAINT TYPES

Water based paints

The following water-based paints are thinned with water and can be coloured with universal stainers, artists' acrylic, gouache or powder colours, all of which are soluble in water.

Vinyl matt—an emulsion paint which gives a tough, washable no-shine finish, easily applied, makes a good base for sponging, stencils, brushy colourwashing.

Vinyl silk—smooth emulsion paint which dries with a soft sheen. Its slippery texture makes it suitable for rubbed colour finishes, while its relative non-porosity makes it a cheaper and more easily applied substitute for the eggshell paint suggested as base coat for most of these decorative paint finishes.

Acrylic primer—very fast drying, chalky-textured priming coat for bare wood.

Oil-based paints

All the following paints contain natural oil and are thinned with white spirit. They can be tinted with universal stainer, dissolved in white spirit, or with artists' oil colours in tubes.

Standard undercoat—used after primer and before top coats on woodwork. Dries with a matt, powdery finish which some people like to stencil on, though it needs a matt varnish to toughen it for use.

'Flat' or 'matt' oil-based paint— a specialist paint obtainable from decorators' suppliers, which dries with a matt but smooth finish. It is ideal for painting panelling, antique furniture, and old places or things generally, because its texture is close to paints used a century or more ago.

WALL PAINT FINISHES

Distressed paint finishes are achieved by manipulating wet paint over walls to create a variety of 'special effects': peppered with flecks of colour, as in stippling; neatly striated, as in dragging; or purposefully smudged with a loose bundle of rag, as in ragging. This trio are somewhat formal looking, regularly irregular in effect and look best with polished furniture, good pictures, proper curtains and the air of a discreetly wealthy establishment.

In all these finishes the paint used is not straight paint out of the tin, but paint much thinned or made flexible with scumble glaze, or in some cases little more than a thin watery wash of colour. Instead of aiming for thick solid colour, the idea in every case is to tease it out, make it softly blurry and so transparent that the base coat shows through, lighting up the overall effect. In most cases I would advise using these glazes or washes over a pale off-white, cream or perhaps light grey paint applied directly to the wall or on to lining paper. With experience, you may try one colour on top of another, which looks superb and painterly, when it comes off, but needs confidence.

How close the wall texture is to that of a baby's bottom is up to you. A first-class finish, smooth, shadowless and even, is a joy to work on and lends crispness and delicacy to the finish, as well as making it more durable. Applying glazes and washes over ruggedly uneven walls is bound to make for uneven tone, but to many eyes that is especially charming, essential if the room is to look more like a decaying *palazzo* than a chic bandbox. For perfect, even walls, any filling must be sanded smoothly and painted over with base coat not once but twice, to prevent it soaking up the glaze colour and emerging as a blob of strong colour on your delicately cloudy walls. The ideal base to work on, in most cases, is oil-based eggshell paint (e.g. Dulux silthane silk) which is slow and sticky to apply and relatively expensive over a large surface. But it is tough, durable and, because it is non-porous, silk allows surface glazes to be manipulated with greater freedom and delicacy. I find that vinyl silk, which goes on rather easier, makes a fair substitute.

COLOUR

It is nearly always possible to find the colour you want ready mixed in a commercial paint range. Many people prefer to do this. If you only need a little of one colour, for stencilling or painting lines, check out any leftover paints you may have. Odds and ends of coloured emulsions can be paled down by adding white emulsion, or intermixed for a new colour. Decorators generally mix up their own colours on the spot using appropriate tinting media—artists' oil colour, acrylics, gouache, powder colours or universal stainers—whichever is appropriate for the type of paint chosen. One colour man claims he can get any colour by intermixing the fairly limited basic shades available in universal stainers, extra concentrated tints which have the advantage that they can be used to colour oil-based and water-based paints.

If you decide to mix your own colours, start with a range of these colours—the basic primaries like red, blue and yellow plus black and raw umber will take you a long way, colourwise. Mixing these into a white base in various combinations, shadowing with a touch of black, or mellowing with raw umber, will give you a large range of the paler colours. For dark colours, find a colour close to the one you want on the manufacturer's colour chart, adding a little of the appropriate stainer to adjust it.

Some colours prove elusive, so pure or subtle that the stainers just miss being right. Artists' colours (oils, acrylics, gouache or powders according to the type of paint) are the solution, coming in a huge range of colours, from delicate to brilliant.

The rule is to use water-based tinting colour with water-based paints, oil-based tinting colour with oil-based paints (see paint identification chart). Universal stainers can be used with both. Start by dissolving the tint colour in very small amounts of the appropriate solvent, using a stubby artists' brush and stir this into a small amount of the base paint. This is a sample colour, which you may want to modify by adding other colours. Note which colours you are using, in roughly what proportions. When you hit the shade you want, go ahead and mix up enough tinting agent to colour the entire tin of base paint. Remember colours always look stronger used over a large area.

People often complain that, whatever colours they start out with, they always end up with mud. This comes from intermixing too many strong primary or complementary colours, so they cancel each other out. The answer here is to go carefully, adding a little of this or that.

QUANTITIES

The decorative finishes described here use very little orthodox paint. Half a litre of standard paint is enough for an average-sized room, because the paint is stretched with water or white spirit. Until you have had a little practice, it is best to start on the wall which will be least noticeable—usually the window wall. That way beginner's uncertainty will not be on display. On the other hand, don't get uptight about doing them, there is nothing here that you cannot speedily pick up if you set your mind to it. Always begin in one corner and leave off in another as joins half-way across a wall are rather noticeable. Once you get into the rhythm of these finishes they go very quickly, absolutely belt along where there are two of you—like rag-rolling a tall Georgian room in four hours.

It is sensible to keep a note of your paint formula in every new instance, so that you can re-mix it if necessary. Precise measurements of the colours used are not necessary, just rough proportions—one inch burnt sienna, half inch raw umber, half inch yellow ochre. Any left-over glaze too should be decanted into a screw-top jar, for touching-up operations. But remember to stir it up thoroughly before use and test a little—you may find the thinner has evaporated, and the colour has darkened. If so, add more thinner. There is no need to varnish over oil-based glazed finishes, as these dry hard enough over a few weeks to be washed down carefully when necessary. On the other hand, coats of varnish can have a pleasing effect, if they are sanded down between coats, giving great depth and richness to the wall colour and, of course, a tough surface which will last for years. Matt emulsion, colour-washed or sponged walls are not so tough. They can be given an emulsion glaze coat to provide some protection or you can simply resign yourself to repainting in a couple of years for the pleasure of having your walls meanwhile quite flat, matt and non-reflective.

Eggshell—the generic name for a midsheen finish in oil-based paints. Eggshell paints are slower in application than water-based midsheen paints, and need more brushing out, but they give a sleek, tough, porcelain texture to walls and woodwork which makes the ideal base for most decorative paint finishes. Silthane silk is the Dulux version of an eggshell oil-based paint.

Gloss finish—the most widely used oil-based paint, dries with a tough, shiny surface which can be brought to an almost lacquer-like smoothness by repeated rubbing or sanding down of successive coats. Usually used on woodwork or furniture, because of its hard-wearing qualities, but makes a chic, shiny wall finish if the walls are scrupulously filled and levelled first, and sanded between coats

Spray paints

Car spray paints, which people use for both stencilling and furniture finishing, are unusual in having a special thinner, similar to lighter fluid, which is purchasable at point of sale. Under dust-free conditions these give a fine, near flawless—untouched by hand—finish for furniture and knick-knacks. They come in a wide range of colours. Professional stencillers like Lynn le Grice often use spray paints for speeding work up, and achieving a subtly shaded and rounded look by spraying one colour on top of another.

Scumble or transparent oil glaze

Not a paint so much as a transparent vehicle for colour, scumble glaze looks like fluffy honey in the tin, and is much used for decorative paint finishes whether with colour, or mixed with a little oil-based paint+colour, for a softer effect. Because of its composition—some beeswax, linseed oil among other things—it retards the drying of the thin tinted glazes used in many decorative paint finishes, and at the same time takes the imprints of rags, stippling brushes, etc very distinctly. It dries slowly, but is tough enough to be wiped down after two or three weeks, though not as tough a finish as either a solid paint or a varnish. It tends to yellow (in time) thus altering the tone of the glaze like the varnish on an uncleaned Old Master, but this can increase its attractiveness. Sold in specialist paint shops.

157

A dragged finish is best achieved on a smooth wall undercoated with a non-porous oil-based paint.

DRAGGING

As I have already said, for an evenly dragged finish, walls should be smooth in order to achieve an appropriately elegant look. For the best results, dragging — and all the paint finishes in this book — should be applied over a base of flat or mid-sheen oil-based paint, over which the coloured glaze slides on easily and doesn't sink in. Over emulsion, dragging is not so perfectly striped nor does it last so well.

Materials

For best results the walls should be given a base coat of oil-based paint in an eggshell finish. Vinyl silk is a good substitute, as it is reasonably non-porous and smooth. Over this you drag a semi-transparent glaze made up of a little of the base coat paint, a little more of scumble glaze and a great deal of the appropriate thinner, white spirit. Exact proportions can vary according to the porosity of the walls, temperature of the room, but 1 tablespoon of paint to two of glaze to $\frac{3}{4}$ pint of white spirit is a rough guide. The glaze can be tinted with universal stainers, or artists' oil colours. Mix these separately (a couple of inches at a time is plenty, not half the tube) with white spirit, dissolving with a small stiff brush, and add this gradually to the mixed-up glaze till you get the colour you want.

The best brush for dragging, I find, is a four-inch standard decorating brush in a cheaper quality, which means it is not too soft and bushy. Dragging brushes, with extra long flexible bristles, are really for graining effects and too floppy for dragging on walls. Use an ordinary wide paintbrush with a second one for applying the glaze. You should also have a supply of white spirit for thinning glaze, a wide tin, bucket or paint kettle for mixing colour and some rags for wiping the brush. As with all these techniques, you will need a ladder to reach the tops of walls.

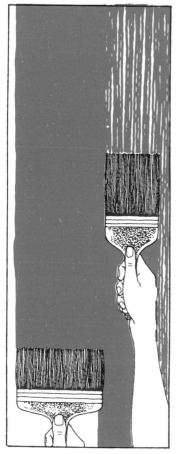

With a wide brush apply a band of colour from top to bottom of the wall, then drag over this with a narrower brush.

Method

Dragging works best with two people, one applying the glaze or wash and the other dragging. The first partner uses a wide brush to apply a narrow band of colour — about 18 inches (45 cm) wide is what experts recommend — the whole height of the wall, keeping the glaze or wash thin or it will tend to run. The second partner then drags *his* brush down with a firm, light, even pressure from top to bottom of the wall. He should take care to relax pressure on the brush at the tops and bottoms of walls as colour may build up here. The dragging brush should be wiped on rags frequently or it will become overloaded. The dragged room should be left for at least two days while it dries and takes on its real colour and tone.

At this point, you can give the dragged finish a coat of varnish — this applies equally to all of the other finishes in this book. Varnish protects the walls from damage, gives them a longer life and makes them washable.

STIPPLING

Stippling suits most varieties of decor as it is soft and unassuming—a mosaic of fine speckles. The finish can be applied by means of a stippling brush or with a roller or a cloth and each gives its own, slightly different effect.

Stippling is best in clear colours over light base coats so that the base shows through to give the glaze a paler, softer colour. It needs smooth walls painted first with undercoat followed by an oil-based coat.

Materials

You will need a transparent oil glaze, and artists' oil colours to tint. As a stippling tool, you can use a special brush, a roller or rags—even screwed-up paper. You should also have white spirit, a bucket or paint kettle, mopping up rags and, as always, a ladder.

Method

The method differs with the tool used. Using a brush gives a very pretty result, but is extremely slow and painstaking. As with dragging, this works best with two people, one brushing on, the other stippling. The stippling brush is applied firmly to the wet glaze and lifts off speckles so the base colour shows through. Again, as with dragging, it is important to work fast, keeping a wet edge of glaze from one stripe of paint to the next, and to clean the brush frequently to avoid any build-up. The same method is used with rags, which must be changed continually to prevent the paint build-up and require a similar sure touch to remove the glaze.

Roller stippling is a fast, comparatively easy method which entails pushing the roller over and over the wet glaze to 'texture' the colour. As with the other methods, avoid a build-up on the roller.

For a longer lasting finish, a coat of varnish can be applied when the colour is quite dry.

To arrive at an even stippled effect (above left) you can use the slow-but-sure stippling brush (top), a stippling rag to lift off the glaze (centre), or the fast roller method (above).

SPONGING ON

Over old paint, poor walls, or rooms which need a quick cheering up, sponging on is a natural and fun to do, easy and speedy. If your colour sense is subtle, you can make sponged effects look like marble. A glance at a marble slab somewhere will give you the basic tones.

Materials

You will need 2 tablespoons of white undercoat, $\frac{3}{4}$ pint (450 ml) of white spirit and enough artists' oil colour to bring it to the shade you want. To mix, spoon the undercoat into a paint kettle or bowl and thin it with $\frac{1}{2}$ pint (300 ml) of white spirit. In a small cup, mix the tube colour—say three inches (7.5 cm)—with enough white spirit to liquify it, stirring hard to dissolve the lumps. Add

159

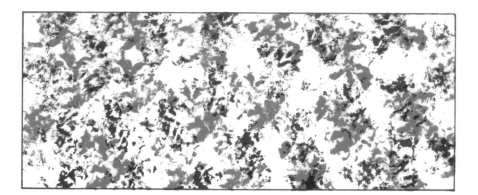

Use a real marine sponge—not plastic foam—to get soft prints when sponging on colour.

Squeeze most of the colour out of the sponge then dab on your first colour (top) followed, when dry, by the next colour (above).

the colour slowly to the thinned undercoat, stirring for at least two to three minutes because it takes time for the blend to be thorough. Try the colour on paper and, if necessary, mix up more concentrated colour and add as before.

You will also need a real sponge—marine not plastic foam—rags to wipe off splatters on woodwork and a stepladder to get to the top of the wall. It is best to keep your paint either in a kettle, stable enough to balance on top of the ladder where you can reach it or on a table near by, protected by newspaper. Also have sheets of newspaper handy to blot up surplus colour.

Method

To sponge, dip the sponge into your thinned colour, squeeze most of it out again and then delicately blob it on the wall. It should make a soft but clear print of colour. If it is too dark, you have too much paint on the sponge. If it is too pale, either add more colour to the mix or prepare to sponge over twice, for more intensity. Once you are happy with colour and print, just keep on dabbing at your wall, lightly but firmly, spacing the prints out a bit, so that some base colour shows through. If it gets a bit heavier here and there, don't fret, a second sponged coat will even it up. Wipe trickles or misses off the woodwork before they set dry. By the time you have completed the room, the first wall will be dry enough to apply another. Sponging usually looks more attractive, softer and more marble, if you sponge on two (or more) colours, as soft as you like, but subtly different—putty with pale pink, greenish-grey with yellow, brown with grey. This way you get a soft build-up of tone and colour, without distinct prints coming through. Leave the walls to dry hard at this point—twenty-four hours will do. Wet colour, especially transparent colour, is misleading. This colour will dry flat, not shiny at all, and look much crisper.

SPONGING OFF

This should perhaps be called 'dabbling around', which is how it feels. In essence, it is the reverse of sponging on. It is a nice easy finish in every way, using emulsion paints only, and suitable for any wall surface or room temperature. Thinned emulsion colour, either straight from the tin or tinted with powder colour or acrylic artists' colour, is brushed on and then broken up with a large marine sponge to create a soft, mottled effect, which dries quite matt and makes a very pleasant background for stencils. Some people prefer very crisp stencils on a plain flat wall colour. I like them a little blurry, unevenly coloured on a softly variegated wall colour, so they look like embroidery.

Materials

You will need approximately 1 part matt emulsion paint to 2 parts water. If

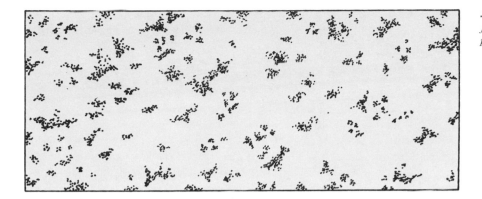

tinting with acrylics or powder colours, mix these to a solution first with water and add gradually to the emulsion and water mix. Both of these types of colour are liable to thicken the mix and make it dry a little faster, so you may need to add more water. On the other hand, if the mixture starts trickling, stir in more emulsion. If you are trying to sponge off over a silk finish emulsion, the mixture may refuse to stick evenly. Adding a tablespoonful of anything in the PVA line, from Copydex to emulsion glaze, will help give it sticking power. Or you could coat the walls first with emulsion glaze. If you want a silky finish, simply use vinyl silk instead of matt emulsion in the recipe.

You will need steps, as usual, a large sponge for 'dabbling', a 5-inch (12.5 cm) decorating brush and rags to clean up.

Cover a strip of wall with thinned emulsion and dabble with a well-rinsed sponge.

Method

Two people make light work of this finish. The painter brushes washy emulsion over a strip of wall, while the sponger follows on dabbling the wet colour all over with the sponge. If the 'wet edge' hardens anywhere, simply sponge lightly with water to soften it, and carry on. That is all there is to it, except to remind you that the sponge will need fairly frequent rinsing and squeezing out in warm water, to prevent it getting too stiff. Wring it out well before carrying on, or it will be too wet, and start dissolving the wash.

COLOUR-WASHING

Anyone of painterly sensibilities will probably enjoy this finish the most. What it should look like is transparent colour laid on criss-cross so that some of the brushwork shows. This gives a lively texture, without being consistent as in a recurring pattern. In warm clear colours, over a white base—the yellow, apricot, peachy range or clear sky blue—the effect is delicate and luminous. This is a great finish with any sort of furnishings except, perhaps, ultra-modern. There are various methods of achieving the effect, which

Colourwashing makes for a luminous, lively wall finish.

161

differs slightly with the paint media used. The first method is the one most people find easiest to manage; the second is messier but the end result is delicately beautiful.

Recipe One Materials
Use artists' oil colour to tint a thinned undercoat solution (see *Sponging On*, page 159). It should be applied over a vinyl silk base if you want a soft brushiness, but it can sometimes go over standard matt emulsion if you add a tablespoonful of scumble glaze to keep the colour workable a moment or two longer. Scumble glaze, which looks like fluffy golden beeswax, is sold in most specialist paint shops these days and is combined with paint glazes to retard setting and keep the solution flexible while taking sharper prints and impressions from brush, rag or whatever.

Recipe One Method
Apply colour-washed colour with a 4–5 inch (10–12.5 cm) decorating brush, in broad, sweeping, loose strokes, criss-crossing here and there. The object is to cover about 85% of the base colour, but not with colour at the same intensity. In some places it should be teased out like a cloud wisp, at others it can be quite vivid and noticeably brushy. Using oil-based colour, one coat may be enough. Leave it twenty-four hours to dry hard. If it is blotchy, rather than dappled, a second coat, applied the same way but concentrating on the lightest areas, will soften and even things up.

Recipe Two
This method gives a luminous colour but is tricky to apply till you get the hang of it and makes a dreadful mess, trickling off the skirtings.

Recipe Two Materials
Use two tablespoonsful of white emulsion, matt or silk finish, diluted in approximately 1 pint (600 ml) water and tinted with artists' gouache colours. Gouache colours are vivid but clear and give wonderful blues and greens and pinks. This is a true wash, being watery colour, and should be applied over matt emulsion or, better still, over acrylic primer which has a blotting-paper surface which will need light sanding beforehand to smooth it a little.

Recipe Two Method
Apply as before, but you will need to coax the colour to stick to the wall, catching the drips as they form and working them back in. Anyone with experience of watercolour painting will not find it alarming though others may, till they get the knack. Better to apply the colour vividly and densely enough to give the effect you want in one application—adding another will probably shift the first a bit, since the emulsion content is so slight. In spite of all these difficulties, it is worth persevering with, because it gives the most beautiful effect.

A very successful colour-washed room I have seen uses diluted powder colour brushed over a base prepared with a mixture of whiting and water painted on in the usual way then left to dry. Old-style distemper paint (now out of production except in Europe), which was always used for colour-washing by decorators because of its pleasing soft matt texture, is only whiting plus water plus enough glue size to bind. I daresay the finish I saw would be soft enough to rub off as it missed out the glue, but a coat of diluted size over the top would help that. Otherwise, if durability were not the chief criterion of the exercise, I would accept its fragility and simply repaint regularly, as the Greek islanders whitewash the steps and hearths of their homes once a week.

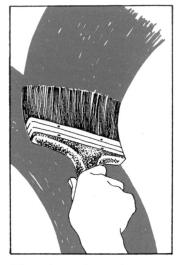

When colourwashing use broad, sweeping criss-crossing strokes with a 4–5 inch (10–12 cm) brush.

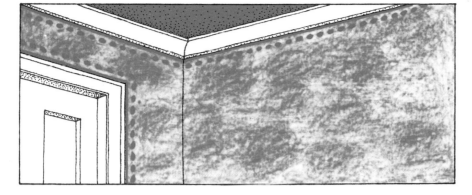

A rubbed colour finish is a great background for stencils.

RUBBED COLOUR

This is so easy it seems a cheat, but it gives a delicate flow of colour, slightly cloudy, a little irregular. It must be applied over a smooth base coat, eggshell or vinyl silk. It makes the perfect background to stencil over, either in an overall pattern or an elaborate border.

Materials

You need artists' oil colours to tint, 1 tablespoonful scumble and $\frac{1}{4}$ pint (150 ml) white spirit. The principle here is that one is rubbing in a highly concentrated version of the colour wanted, but spreading it so thinly that it emerges as a fine gauze of colour—exactly like putting on rouge. Mix up a generous quantity of oil colour to start with and test by rubbing a dab out on white paper. This mix gives clear intense colour. For chalky colour add 1 spoonful of white undercoat. You may need transparent emulsion glaze to fix the first layer before applying the second. Arm yourself with soft, lint-free rags, made by tearing up old sheets, pillow cases or tights. A stepladder, as usual, will be needed for reaching the tops of walls.

Method

Begin in a corner. To apply, dip the rag into colour, bundled up to make a soft wadge in the hand and then start gently rubbing it over the wall, with a circular polishing motion. With care, the colour can be spun out into a perfectly even coat, but as a rule it settles a little more thickly here, thinly there and this gives a faint cloudiness which is very attractive. The one thing to guard against is going over a previously coloured patch, because this tends to shift the previous colour and leave a tide line where the two meet. If you work quite fast, only breaking off when you come to a corner, this should not happen.

As with most of these finishes, a richer effect is obtained by rubbing a second layer of colour over the first. Leave the first coat to set hard. Scumble glaze hardens slowly so this will take three or four days. Then experimentally rub the second colour on top, choosing a corner which won't show. If the second rubbing dislodges the first, you will need to apply a buffer coat of transparent colourless glaze, which dries matt. Emulsion glaze fits the bill perfectly and can be obtained from specialist paint shops. It should be applied with a soft brush, like a varnish. Don't worry about the milky appearance, this clears as it dries. Once dry you can rub away on top safely.

With a rag dipped in the paint, use small circular strokes to 'polish' on the colour.

RAGGING AND RAG-ROLLING

Ragging entails pressing soft, bunched-up rag lightly and firmly into wet glaze to leave a nicely textured print a little reminiscent of fossil marble, without veins. Because the rags keep changing shape a little, and one changes

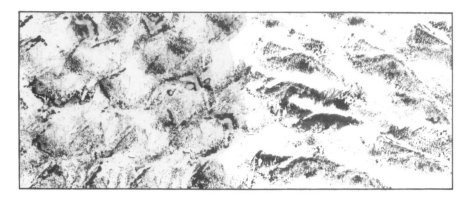

one's ragging direction the whole time, the prints never coalesce into a formal pattern, but flow across the wall with a gentle dappled effect. It is usually most appealing done in soft, clear pastels over a white base, which must be either white eggshell or white vinyl silk, to encourage the glaze to stay wet and printable as long as possible. Very sophisticated effects can be achieved by two separate ragged coats, of gentle harmonizing colours, superimposed. A brown-paper colour ragged on top of a ragged coat of light grey, for instance, looks excellent in a quiet, studious room, with simple polished furniture and prints. A band of plain colour painted on round the edges of the walls tightens up a ragged room visually, and is especially helpful if there is no cornice.

The two techniques differ slightly. Ragging is done with the bunch of rags held loosely in the hand and pressed quickly in all directions—not in tidy rows up and down, which would give a repeating pattern, but over the whole glazed area. Rag-rolling means what it says—a soft bundle of rags is rolled up the wall surface. This gives a more directional effect, but some people find it easier to do.

Ragging and rag-rolling are best done by two people, one applying the glaze over a strip of wall, the other ragging it off. As another strip of wet glaze is brushed on, it overlaps the first slightly, and it is important that the first is not drying off because this leads to a sudden thickening of colour which is difficult to rag. What this means is that both parties have to work fast and in unison, so that the ragger is working about half a minute behind the painter. In the trade, this problem is referred to as 'keeping a wet edge'. Usually, people find painting on a strip about 18 inches (45 cm) wide is the most manageable, but you both need to be adept at weaving in and out of each other's way. A light, rigid aluminium stepladder is a great help. Should the worst happen and a strip of glaze harden too much to rag, the best course is to rub it right off again with a rag moistened with white spirit. Immediately reapply glaze, blending it in with the previously ragged strip, and continue ragging as before. Ragging should be stopped—if you must stop—in a corner or one edge of the chimney breast. This way you can resume work without a telltale build-up of colour at the join between old and new glaze. Glaze which goes on to woodwork or skirtings should be wiped off from time to time with rags moistened in white spirit. It takes several hours for the glaze to set, but the sooner one wipes off marks, the more easily they dissolve. Stray colour on cornice and ceiling is best touched out with emulsion when the job is finished.

When applying a second ragged coat, leave the first to dry really hard first. A week is about right, though the drying may take a few days less in warm weather. Cold weather and a cold room slow up the drying time of the wet glaze, which makes ragging go easier, so it is a good idea to switch off central heating in the room where you are working and keep warm by wearing more thick clothes. On the other hand don't have the room so cold that your hands go numb and you start dropping your rags!

Materials

You will need 1 part white undercoat to approximately $2\frac{1}{2}$ parts white spirit, 1 tablespoonful scumble glaze and artists' oil colours for tinting. The glaze should be painted on with a 4–5 inch (10–12.5 cm) decorating brush. It should not trickle down noticeably after you brush it on—if it does it is too thin, and undercoat and artists' colour should be added. Alternatively, a spoonful more scumble glaze can be added and stirred well to mix. This makes the glaze colour softer.

Method

Starting at the top of the steps by the ceiling line, the painter brushes glaze thinly and fairly evenly (brushmarks don't matter, though don't overdo them, but gaps, 'holidays' as painters say, do) down a strip of wall 18 inches (45 cm) wide, all the way down to the bottom. If the ragger is nimble, he or she can swap places on the step before the painter reaches the bottom, which saves useful minutes. As the ragger rags down towards the skirting, the painter moves the steps on and brushes the glaze over the adjacent strip of wall, just overlapping the two strips to prevent visible joins.

In ragging the rag is bunched up and dabbed over the glaze. In rag-rolling, it is used in a sausage shape, and rolled over and over the glaze. The chief point to remember with ragging is to keep varying the position of your hand, so that the prints change constantly. Also, change rags as soon as they become stiff with glaze. Rags of different texture can give subtly different prints, but make sure that they are all so well washed and broken in that they don't deposit lint, fluff or threads. Soft paper, like kitchen paper, bunched up, is another possibility, but you will probably have to change it more often still. At the end of a wall, stand back and check it for thin spots where the glaze is noticeably weaker. The easiest remedy for these is to rag on colour—pick up a dab of glaze on your rag and lightly touch it over the bald spot. Ragged walls have a tendency to look a bit jumpy when just done and before the glaze has hardened and gone matt. Twenty-four hours later is when you get the full effect.

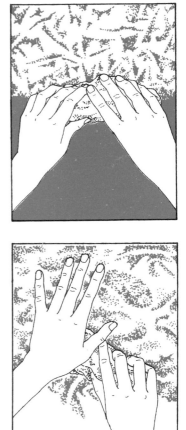

Brush on a strip of glaze and then use a bunched-up rag to dab over the area (top). For a different effect, form the rag into a sausage shape and roll over the glaze (above).

RUBBING OFF

This could also be called 'sanding off'. I hit on it accidentally, trying to even up and lighten an over-enthusiastically rollered-on emulsion paint over a roughly plastered wall. After quite vigorous sanding, the opaque surface layer of paint had been rubbed away, leaving a fine speckly-coloured surface, more tawny than red, which looks like the painted wall surfaces of Pompeii. Because of the sanding the colour is forced into the wall surface (which also becomes wonderfully smooth, a delight to stencil or paint murals on) and it looks ancient, time worn, as much colour stained as painted.

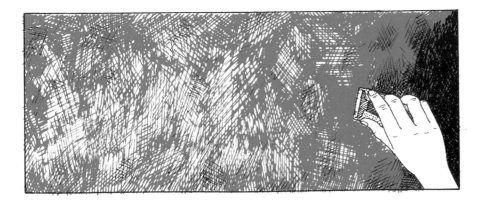

If you sandpaper over a rough emulsioned wall you will get a time-worn effect and a beautifully smooth surface.

Painting Special Effects

There are a few paint tricks which look impressive without being unduly difficult and they are the ones people most often ask about, or spontaneously admire when they see them. Without being particularly grand or elaborate, they add a certain distinction to a room.

FALSE PANELS

Using painted lines—making up squares or rectangles—to suggest panels on plain painted walls is a useful way of correcting a room's proportions and giving a box of a place a more structured look. Too-tall rooms need a horizontal emphasis and this can be achieved by painted lines based on the classical wainscot arrangement of small panels below the dado line and taller ones above. Rooms which need height, on the other hand, get a vertical emphasis from rectangular panels arranged side by side with a space above and below. These panels can be combined with painted or stencilled friezes, or borders to further cut the height or width. The field of the panels can be painted a different colour from the walls or given a decorative finish like marbling for a grandly neo-classical effect. Or, in Thirties style, they can be papered, using a large pictorial design which gives an effect something like panels of painted Chinese silk or wallpaper. Wherever you have too much wall and too little in the way of pictures or mirrors, painted panels like these are a great way of relieving the blankness—halls, stairways, passages, are a good example. They can also be used to visually anchor furniture groupings, or something like a large mirror which seems arbitrary simply floating in the middle of one wall. Compare the two photographs of my sitting-room (pages 56–57) and you will see how painting blue lines either side of the mirror behind the divan ties it into the room and provides a visual justification for its presence there.

The first step is to work out what size and arrangement of panels best suits your room and how wide the painted lines should be. The easiest way to do this is to cut long strips of coloured paper and Blu-tack or pin them in place to judge the effect. The panels should be the same size wherever they occur in an unbroken run, though narrower panels can be located where the architecture of the room seem to justify it, between two long windows, for instance. Smaller panels can go above a doorway, but the top and bottom lines must remain the same all the way round. Where the ceiling line or the floor slopes, the best solution is to trust your eye, and go for the arrangement which looks convincing, even if it is not exactly square to the ceiling or floor. If painting on lines seems like too much work, you can simply paste down the strips of coloured paper to outline panels, perhaps using marbled paper. The advantage of the painted lines is that they look more integrated and last longer.

Materials

You will need a steel straight edge or straight wooden batten, a pencil, measuring tape, a plumb line (this can be a weight tied to a long piece of twine), Blu-tack, coloured paper, scissors, emulsion paint plus acrylic colours for tinting, a small square-ended artist's brush for outlining and a half- or one-inch standard decorating brush for filling in.

Method

Work out the best size and disposition of panels for the room, as above. Leave equal spaces between the panels either side of door and window frames—don't overcrowd them. The space above and below the panels is something to be gauged by experiment, shifting your strips till the arrangement looks convincing. When you have worked out the basic module which can be repeated round the walls with the minimum of adaptation, you can start measuring and pencilling the panel lines directly on to the walls. Use a plumb line to find the true vertical, standing on a chair or table and suspending the weighted string from the ceiling line—when it stops swinging get someone to mark the vertical lightly with pencil or chalk. Pencil all outlines lightly, in case you make a mistake. Mix up the paint colour by adding a little water to the acrylic tinting colours (artists' acrylic colours from artists' supply shops) and then mixing this very thoroughly into a little matt emulsion paint in a cup. I find a cup with a handle is the easiest paint container to use where one is running up and down a step ladder or jumping on and off a chair. If you are worried about running out of paint, and not being able to match the colour again, mix up a generous amount and decant this into the cup as you need it.

Use the small artist's brush to paint in the outer edge of your lines first. A wooden batten, half an inch thick, can be helpful for steadying your brush, but only use it to rest your hand on—painting close up to the edge, as if you were ruling a line with a pencil, will lead to smudging when you move the batten. Any blobs or smudges should be wiped off immediately with a damp rag. But don't get too worried about getting lines mathematically straight—a slight wavering here and there won't show up in the final effect. Having outlined the panel lines, simply fill in with the standard brush and leave to dry. It's only a detail, but I find that on walls with a special finish, like the rubbed on colour of my sitting-room, that distressing the painted lines to give a similarly broken colour effect looks better. The flat blue lines we started out with looked too hard against the cloudy pink. To distress the blue, I mixed up a sludgy version of the basic blue, adding burnt umber, and just brushed this a bit haphazardly over the basic blue, rubbing it in with my finger.

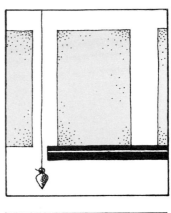

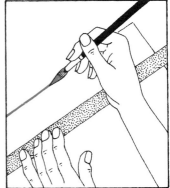

To position 'false panels' cut strips of coloured paper and tack or sellotape to walls to find the best arrangement. Use a plumb-line to check verticals (top). Then pencil round as a guide and paint in outlines $\frac{1}{2}$–1 inch (1–2 cm) wide with a pointed artist's brush (above).

FAKE 'ASHLAR' COURSING

The idea behind this effect is to suggest, very lightly, the look of stone walls built of equal-sized blocks with edges chiselled off at an angle to create a V-shaped groove when the blocks are assembled. There was a vogue for this in classical revival circles, at the beginning of the nineteenth century. I found a fake ashlar wallpaper, boldly printed in white and sepia on to thick parchment-coloured paper, on the walls of the hall and staircase in my own Regency house. The paper was in such a tattered state it had to go but I decided to copy the effect in paint (see page 118), because I felt the slight strictness of the pattern suited the simplicity of the architecture.

Materials

You will need steps or a stool to stand on, a straight edge to rule with and a pencil. Two fine-pointed sable brushes and one narrow blunt-cut one will be required, together with white undercoat, raw umber and burnt umber artists'

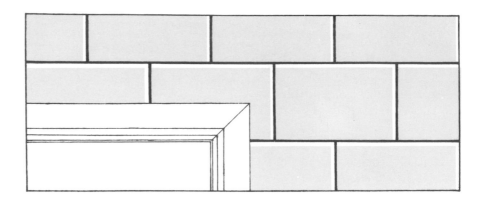

The finished 'ashlar' effect should be one of walls made of stone blocks.

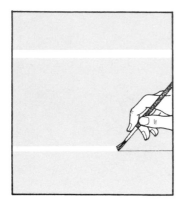

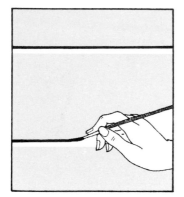

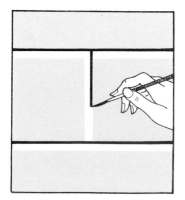

First paint over your pencilled marker lines in white using a blunt-cut brush (top); make a sepia shadow line with a pointed sable brush (centre) before adding the vertical lines (above).

oil colours, clear varnish and white spirit. You should also have to hand rags to wipe off mistakes and a measuring tape.

Method

The walls should previously be given a finish that vaguely resembles stone, creamy coloured or yellowish. Mine were done by brushing (see *Colour-washing*, pages 161–162) thinned vinyl silk emulsion tinted with a little raw sienna and raw umber acrylic colour over an ivory vinyl silk base. The colour-washing looked quite rough to begin with, but strangely, as soon as the fake stonework was painted on top, precisely dividing and subdividing the surface, all the slightly erratic brushmarks and splodges 'read' as convincingly stained and discoloured stone. In an old house, like mine, nothing is quite straight, vertically or horizontally. In similar situations, check measured lines with your eye before painting them in, because often what looks right will be more convincing than what is accurate according to the tape.

Ashlar blocks can be any size, in theory, but are always rectangular, and look sensible in a modest building like mine in blocks 14 × 10 inches (35 × 25 cm). If possible, try to work out a size that allows the wall to be sectioned into equal widths all the way down—a half course of stone at top or bottom looks as if the stonemasons hadn't done their homework. Using steel tape and straight edge, lightly pencil in all the horizontal courses. The vertical lines are easy, once you have measured off one course, because the join between two blocks comes half-way across the block above, and so on. Some people find it easier and quicker to measure and cut a template in thick card, fractionally smaller than the block, and pencil round this each time. Wrong pencil lines can be removed with bread, soft erasers or a soapy rag.

The first step is to paint over all the pencil lines in white or off-white. To do this, mix up some white undercoat, a little varnish and some white spirit in a cup to a thin cream consistency, thick enough to give opacity and coverage, thin enough to flow nicely. Using the blunt-cut brush paint lines just under $\frac{1}{2}$ inch (1 cm) wide over all the pencilled guidelines. When these have dried hard, mix up a sepia colour for the shadowed effect, using raw umber or a dot of burnt umber in varnish, with very little white spirit indeed. This colour needs to flow smoothly, but must not seep or 'move'. Using a fine sable brush, paint the shadow line over the white. Wobbles and swerves can be wiped off speedily with rag moistened with white spirit. My 'ashlar' barely does more than hint at the grooving, because my hall is too small to cope with dramatic illusions, but people with larger, loftier rooms can experiment with a much bolder handling of the shadows suggested by thinning and thickening the dark lines, and mitring where they meet at the corners. Either way the effect is good. I wish now that I had varnished my ashlar walls because with constant brushing against and running past, their crispness is diminishing gradually and varnished walls can be washed down quite safely.

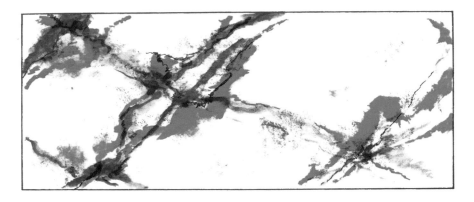

A lively approximation of marble can be rendered in paint with a little practice.

MARBLING

This is not intended to deceive anyone, but makes an interestingly varied and lively finish for woodwork, floors, in fact anything you would like a little variegated. Marbling looks rich. The boldest marbled effects are often the most successful, quite strong veining with definite pebbles of colour. The greatest help is to have a slab of good marble to hand as a visual reference and reminder of Nature's infinite versatility. The principle behind this sort of sketchy marbling is that you are squiggling two or three darker colours, the veins, into a still wet grey glaze, and then softening these by lightly brushing or sponging them. Highlights and so on can be added when this is dry. Nothing could be simpler, in theory. In practice, it hangs on how skilfully varied and spontaneous your squiggly veining looks, both in a small section and overall. Don't worry, though, with a length of skirting's practice you will have fallen into the swing of it.

Materials

The base for greyish marbling should be white eggshell paint, lightly smoothed over with fine sandpaper. You will then need white undercoat, white spirit, raw umber and black artists' oil colour, clear polyurethane varnish, fine pointed sable brushes, a soft decorator's brush and a small sponge and rags.

Method

Mix up a greenish-grey glaze using raw umber and a little black oil colour mixed into undercoat thinned 2 to 1 with white spirit. Brush this over a section of woodwork. Break it up by sponging lightly. With a small brush dipped in brown-grey, feather in (some people use real feathers instead of brushes) diagonal lines intersecting from time to time—a bit like a road map. With the soft paint brush, stroke back and forth very lightly across these veins to soften and smudge them a little. Now add more lines, blacker ones, linking the first together to make 'pebbles' or following beside them a little way then branching off. Soften these lines, too. With a soft rag, stipple flecks of grey and brown and black here and there. Finally, soften the whole area you have just marbled by taking the brush gently back and forth along the veins to smudge them. When this is dry, it will look very soft. Now is the moment to harden it up, with tiny black feathery lines added here and there, white squiggles and the odd 'pebble', best done with colour made transparent with a little varnish. When hard, dry varnish twice with clear polyurethane, semi-gloss or gloss. This should be lightly rubbed over when dry too, to cut the shine a little and give the cool smooth texture of marble. On a floor, varnish at least four times.

Much more dramatic 'marbles' can be simulated by painting with light colours on to a dark base. Nigel Coates's impressive midnight-blue doorways

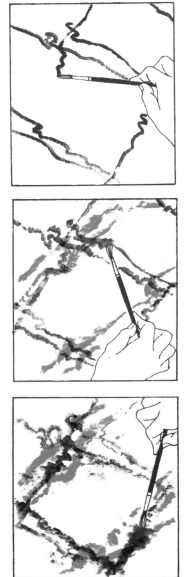

'Feather' in diagonal lines over a previously sponged surface (top). Stroke the lines with a brush to smudge them (centre). Add squiggly darker lines and white lines to intersect with your first ones (above).

169

and pediments were marbled, with a slightly bolder approach—thicker lines and veins, larger pebbles—in shades of blue over black and highlights in off-white grey and pale blue.

If marbling appeals to you, and you want to try for a more *faux marbre* finish, which is more convincing, you could do worse than copy real chunks of marble in the colours and formations you most enjoy. The main difference between the sketchy version and the painstaking one is that the latter makes more use of transparency, colour floated on in varnish, left to dry, then more floated on top. As you can imagine, this counterfeits the crystalline depth of colour in the real stone. There are many books on this technique (see *Bibliography*).

When marbling a floor, always section it off into squares or lozenges, manageable sections in other words. Not only does this make the marbling go faster, it gives a more varied effect in the end because each square will tend to be a little different. Outline each section in black paint, with small black diamond insets, if you like.

FAKE GRAINING

The wildest graining one sees is always the best. It saddens me that skilled grainers should spend months working on a pine door to make it pass for oak, when it would look better left as pine or painted plain colours. Grainer's 'oak' is yellow and sickly, though a marvel of dissimulation and technique. The only graining worth having, in my view, is something like the oyster walnut graining at Ham House, Richmond, or the wayward and dramatically squiggled fake walnut Dennis Severs painted over a small panelled room he uses as a smoking room American colonial style (see page 33).

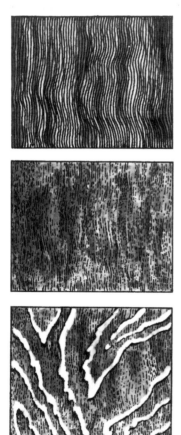

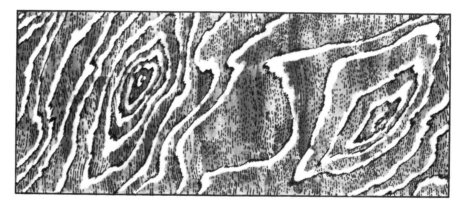

To arrive at a convincing grainy look first drag a dry brush over the wet glaze (top), with a soft, clean brush gently blur the lines (above centre), draw heart wood lines on the wet glaze with the edge of a cork (above) and, in the same way, draw a knot shape (above right).

Dennis used scumble glaze tinted a middling brown to colour his cream painted panelling. Over this, when dry, he used a darker brown, shading into black here and there, to comb, pounce (with a cork) and press (with string) all manner of woody motifs. Looked at close to, it is more eccentric than even oyster walnut, but seen as a whole, it has the vitality and exuberance of grained New England interiors, where the colours and marks are so bold and unexpected it is sometimes hard to know whether this is meant to be wood or marble. It is wonderful either way.

SPRAY LACE

The best lace to use for this technique is one with a large pattern surrounded by open mesh areas. Madras cotton lace (available at good department stores by the yard) is ideal, since the patterned areas, usually floral, are dense enough to block the spray whereas the mesh in the invervening areas is open

An instant brocaded look to a wall or other surface (far left) is achieved by spraying paint through a piece of lace sellotaped in place (left).

enough to let it through clearly. What happens when you spray paint through the stretched-out lace is that the lace design emerges negatively. If you spray white paint over a pink ground, in other words, the pattern will emerge as pink flowers on a white ground.

Materials

You will need cans of aerosol car spray paint (available from ironmongers, DIY stores and motor supply shops) and a piece of coarse cotton lace. Make sure the room is well ventilated while spraying.

Method

Stretch the lace over the area to be patterned, sellotaping or stapling it in place. Then, holding the paint can as instructed—generally, vertically and at a distance of about a foot—spray evenly over the area. Leave for a few seconds, then remove the lace. Patterning a large area can cause problems with pattern repeats unless you take great care. For a large drop of wall, it would pay you to buy a length of lace as long as the wall itself, overlapping the selvedges as you go along so that the pattern matches up horizontally as well as vertically.

STENCILS

A stencil is a means of reproducing a decorative pattern quickly and accurately by hand. Before machines could do anything quicker, stencilling was used for speed. Now it is enjoying a considerable revival because it looks so attractive and because you don't have to be anything like a talented artist to produce sensationally pretty effects.

Stencils can be used to add pattern and colour to almost anything around you which could do with brightening up. You can stencil walls, floors, units, furniture, stair treads, trays, boxes, lampshades, even fabrics. Using stencils, you can add painted borders, little calico print patterns, or large bold motifs. It all depends on how you cut your stencil.

Commercial stencils, either printed on stencil card for you to cut or ready-cut, are available in a modest variety of designs, mostly folksy, birds, floral motifs, willow trees. If your taste runs to something different it is not difficult, and much more fun, to cut one's own stencils. Not all designs or motifs can be transposed straight into stencil shape, for the simple reason that without 'ties' at strategic points, the entire design falls out of the card leaving a pretty-shaped hole, but no detail. With a little experiment, most designs can be adapted, but there are books of printed stencil designs which only need to be traced off and cut, or in some cases enlarged (use a Grant projector, or get a photographic enlargement made to your required size—cheap and much less tedious than scaling up by hand on the grid system).

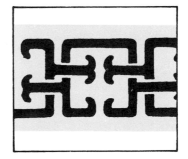

Stencil designs can be adapted from all kinds of sources—samplers, embroidery, tiles, carvings.

171

Some further ideas for stencil shapes (right).

Trace off design to a card using carbon paper.

Cut out the shapes with a scalpel or Stanley knife.

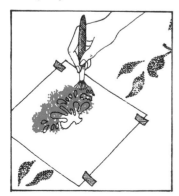

Stipple on a second colour with a coarse brush, fixing the stencil in position with sticky tape.

Materials

The actual stencil can be made from any reasonably tough, waterproofed paper or card—varnished manilla paper is easy to cut, stencil board is strong and not expensive. Use paper for finely detailed small-scale patterns, board for larger motifs. Use carbon paper to trace off designs. The cutting is best done with a small craft knife or scalpel, though a Stanley knife is adequate, too. Lay the stencil on a sheet of plate glass; holding the knife at a slight angle, slice smoothly round the pattern units. Rough jags can be trimmed off.

Other equipment needed includes stencil brushes (ends chopped off straight, usually made of bristle), fast-drying water-based paint colours, saucers for mixing colours, plenty of rags. Water-based acrylic colours have the advantage over oil colours of drying almost instantly—no smudging—and being very transparent in a diluted form, which allows a great range of shading in your stencil.

Method

Mix up the colour you are using first with enough water to make it about the thickness of salad cream. Don't squeeze the whole tube into your saucer. Acrylics dry so fast and stencilling uses so little paint, that this would work out needlessly extravagant. Pick up a little colour on the tips of the bristles of your brush and on a sheet of waste paper jab the bristles firmly and sharply to distribute the colour and work off excess paint.

Large stencils may need to be fixed to the wall with Blu-tack, sellotape or tacks while you work on them. Small ones can usually be held down with one hand while you stencil with the other, and this saves holes in the walls and bald patches where the tape may peel off wall paint. If you are using several colours, the rule is to stencil one colour at a time. Complete the design right round the room, then start over again with colour two, and so on.

By the time you have completed one wall section, you will be familiar with the different effects achieved by using less colour, or shading by means of pounding harder and longer on some areas of the design than others. Never use too much colour on your brush; this gives crude, splodged-looking stencils. On the other hand, don't worry too much about the odd smudge or unevenness in colour, or downright mistakes—these may look glaring in close-up but small mistakes vanish in the overall effect, and colour that varies in intensity gives a lively hand-made look which is an important element in the stencil look. By using the faintest, most transparent colour, you get the effect of old, faded fabric prints, which looks prettier to me than a stronger hard-edged pattern and is particularly winning in one colour on top of another (soft red on pale blue or cream, green over yellow and so on). I also prefer the background colour for stencils to be distressed—sponged or stippled or colour-washed. A slightly varied background gives stencils much more depth, something of the look of old embroidery.

172

italic indicates illustration

The publishers would like to thank the following for their assistance and their permission to use the photographs reproduced in this book:

The American Museum in Britain, Bath 38, 43; Jane Baldwin 72; Peter Bosch 135; Pierre Boulat 13; Simon Brown 2–3, 16, 18–21, 24–25, 27–28, 30, 34, 42, 46, 48–50, 52–54, 56–57, 59, 70–71, 76–78, 82, 84–86, 88–89, 91, 93–94, 96, 98, 101, 106, 109, 111–112, 115, 118, 120, 123, 125, 127–128, 131–132, 134; Ken Druse 138; Dulux 102, 105, 130; Polly Hope 66, 110, 140; Vincent Lisanti 39; Bill McLaughlin 114, 116; Philip McLean 45; Tim Mercer 32, 81, 92; The Royal Pavilion, Art Gallery and Museums, Brighton 22, 44; Alan Short 74; The Trustees of Sir John Soane's Museum 14; Sotheby Parke Burnet & Co 62; Joe Standart 36; Roger Stowell 64; Transglobe 10; Mark Turner, Keeper of the Silver Studio Collection, Middlesex Polytechnic 31; The Victorian Society 67; James Wedge 6, 33, 60, 68, 90, 108.